# Tall Ears and Short Tales

# Tall Ears and Short Tales

✦

## Observations from the Barn

*Carol M. Chapman*
*Foreword by Jerry Finch*
*Afterword by Chris Heyde*

iUniverse, Inc.
New York Lincoln Shanghai

# Tall Ears and Short Tales
**Observations from the Barn**

All Rights Reserved © 2003 by Carol M. Chapman

No part of this book may be reproduced or transmitted in any form or by any means, graphic, electronic, or mechanical, including photocopying, recording, taping, or by any information storage retrieval system, without the written permission of the publisher.

iUniverse, Inc.

For information address:
iUniverse, Inc.
2021 Pine Lake Road, Suite 100
Lincoln, NE 68512
www.iuniverse.com

ISBN: 0-595-28935-5 (pbk)
ISBN: 0-595-74923-2 (cloth)

Printed in the United States of America

# *Dedication*

So many books contain a laundry list of people to thank on this page. It sometimes reminds me of national award shows where everyone from one's baby nurse to the current hairdresser is mentioned as contributing to the success of whatever the award is for. It makes the show run awfully long, especially for us viewers who really want to see only what the attendees are wearing on the show. Other than my mother, no one else on this dedication list has changed my diapers, and my hairdressing is done by the wind and the rain, so my list should go shorter for all you impatient people out there.

This book is lovingly dedicated to my mother. A true artist, she paints life in all its multihued glory for others to wonder over.

This book is humbly dedicated to my father. He took the palette my mother supplied and splashed vivid shades of meaning across my existence.

This book is happily dedicated to all the animals that have shared the wonder of their existence with me.

This book would still be a dream without the generosity of spirit that is Joyce, the careful snipping of threads and dispensing of knowledge by Gary, the graceful turn of Gary-Bob's paw as he pointed out spelling challenges, and Chipper's ever-present-nose.

A large part of the success of my last few years has been attributed to the wonderful company I work for—the American National Insurance Company—and to the management and employees who create a family for me there. That certainly has to be added as part of this dedication. Thank you all.

This book is dedicated to my husband. He has always been there for me and shouldered the burdens of caring for our animals, side by side with me. And if I don't mention him, I'll have to suffer the wrath of a slighted male.

This book is completely filled with the spirit of all those who share this glorious bus ride through life with me.

# Contents

Foreword . . . . . . . . . . . . . . . . . . . . . . . . . . . . . . . . . . . . . xi
Introduction . . . . . . . . . . . . . . . . . . . . . . . . . . . . . . . . . xiii
In the Beginning . . . . . . . . . . . . . . . . . . . . . . . . . . . . . . . . . 1
Horse Ears, Tails, and Everything in Between . . . . . . . . . . . . . . . . 3
Westward How? . . . . . . . . . . . . . . . . . . . . . . . . . . . . . . . . . 5
GoWyeth . . . . . . . . . . . . . . . . . . . . . . . . . . . . . . . . . . . . . 9
Cindy Lou, Where Are You? . . . . . . . . . . . . . . . . . . . . . . . . . 13
Viewing Responsibility through Rose-Colored Glasses . . . . . . . . . 16
Short Tails . . . . . . . . . . . . . . . . . . . . . . . . . . . . . . . . . . . . 19
New Names Are the Stepping Stones to the Future . . . . . . . . . . . . 21
Tall Ears—the Coming of the IRS Drug Mules . . . . . . . . . . . . . . 23
(Official Version, according to Press Releases)
The Coming of the IRS Drug Mules . . . . . . . . . . . . . . . . . . . . 26
(Actual Events Uncovered)
Of Goats and Gardens . . . . . . . . . . . . . . . . . . . . . . . . . . . . 29
You Named a Horse after a Vampire? . . . . . . . . . . . . . . . . . . . 31
Tasmanian Hooligan . . . . . . . . . . . . . . . . . . . . . . . . . . . . . 34
The Fine Art of Stain Removal and Other Horse Ownership
    Facts . . . . . . . . . . . . . . . . . . . . . . . . . . . . . . . . . . . . . 36
Silhouettes in the Noonday Haze . . . . . . . . . . . . . . . . . . . . . . 39

Credo . . . . . . . . . . . . . . . . . . . . . . . . . . . . . . . . . . . . . . . . . . . . . 41
Each Horse's Death Diminishes Me . . . . . . . . . . . . . . . . . . . . . . . 44
The Bison . . . . . . . . . . . . . . . . . . . . . . . . . . . . . . . . . . . . . . . . 51
A Home for Star . . . . . . . . . . . . . . . . . . . . . . . . . . . . . . . . . . . 53
Barn Dreams . . . . . . . . . . . . . . . . . . . . . . . . . . . . . . . . . . . . . . 57
Mud Season . . . . . . . . . . . . . . . . . . . . . . . . . . . . . . . . . . . . . . . 59
Clock Watching . . . . . . . . . . . . . . . . . . . . . . . . . . . . . . . . . . . . 61
Heave Ho . . . . . . . . . . . . . . . . . . . . . . . . . . . . . . . . . . . . . . . . 63
Pretty Is as Pretty Does . . . . . . . . . . . . . . . . . . . . . . . . . . . . . . 65
Enrichment Comes in Many Forms—Some with Legs . . . . . . . . . . 68
Horse Tales . . . . . . . . . . . . . . . . . . . . . . . . . . . . . . . . . . . . . . . 70
Doggone Tales . . . . . . . . . . . . . . . . . . . . . . . . . . . . . . . . . . . . . 73
Quit Poking—I'm Typing . . . . . . . . . . . . . . . . . . . . . . . . . . . . . 74
Diet? Do You Want Me to Die? . . . . . . . . . . . . . . . . . . . . . . . . 76
Doggone Daze . . . . . . . . . . . . . . . . . . . . . . . . . . . . . . . . . . . . . 78
You Did It Now, Chip . . . . . . . . . . . . . . . . . . . . . . . . . . . . . . . 81
Doggone Truths . . . . . . . . . . . . . . . . . . . . . . . . . . . . . . . . . . . . 83
Hard Choices and No Easy Answers . . . . . . . . . . . . . . . . . . . . . 85
Short Tales from Times Gone By . . . . . . . . . . . . . . . . . . . . . . . . 87
My Mother Is an Artist . . . . . . . . . . . . . . . . . . . . . . . . . . . . . . 88
Casual Acts of Kindness . . . . . . . . . . . . . . . . . . . . . . . . . . . . . . 90
Riding the Bus . . . . . . . . . . . . . . . . . . . . . . . . . . . . . . . . . . . . . 92
Time . . . . . . . . . . . . . . . . . . . . . . . . . . . . . . . . . . . . . . . . . . . . 94
Sometimes I Remember and Smile . . . . . . . . . . . . . . . . . . . . . . . 96
Poetry in Motion . . . . . . . . . . . . . . . . . . . . . . . . . . . . . . . . . . . 99

Gabby (A Small Morality Play) . . . . . . . . . . . . . . . . . . . . . . . . 101
The Many Shades of Gratitude . . . . . . . . . . . . . . . . . . . . . . 103
Humor . . . . . . . . . . . . . . . . . . . . . . . . . . . . . . . . . . . . . . . . 105
Whoa . . . . . . . . . . . . . . . . . . . . . . . . . . . . . . . . . . . . . . . . . 107
All Horses Are Brown, Aren't They? . . . . . . . . . . . . . . . . . . 109
Sanctuary . . . . . . . . . . . . . . . . . . . . . . . . . . . . . . . . . . . . . 112
On the Porch . . . . . . . . . . . . . . . . . . . . . . . . . . . . . . . . . . 114
Glossary . . . . . . . . . . . . . . . . . . . . . . . . . . . . . . . . . . . . . . 115
Afterword: Ending a National Disgrace . . . . . . . . . . . . . . . 119

# *Foreword*

In the last thirty years, a miracle has taken place in the world of animal-to-human interaction. Inspired by the works of Tom Dorrance, the days of the rough breaking, "ride 'em till they drop" attitude of horse owners has evolved into a softer and much gentler approach.. Stronger animal cruelty laws and more effective spay/neuter programs reflect the evolution of change in our attitude toward all animals. Circus and zoo animals are far better protected than ever before, thanks to the watchful eyes of the public.

Long before the current change began, Carol Chapman stood as one of the few who saw animals not as objects over which humans have dominion, but as kindred souls on a mutual passage through our life experience. As the child of a widely traveled military family, her first introduction to animal cruelty came from lessons taught to her by a carriage horse.

Through his eyes, she felt the pain and agony of abused animals and, in his memory, she began the long fight for their right not only to live, but also to be understood, respected, and loved.

In her battle against the tide of the common belief that animals are nothing more than tools to be used and thrown away, Carol began to change the minds of those around her by showing them the incredible life of animals and their capacity to share their emotional life with humans.

As one who fights bravely for the humane existence of animals, Carol continues to gather a large following of supporters. Together, they've traveled the halls of federal, state, and local governments to stop the wholesale slaughter of horses. She's battled in the political arena for more humane treatment of pets and, like any true soldier, she carries the wounds of battles lost, wounds that never heal, as she watched animal after animal suffer at the hands of man.

Tackling problems with an international scope becomes overwhelming for any person, especially when the answers involve reaching into the hearts of mankind and asking them touch the soul of an animal, something that must happen before attitudes and laws are changed. Through her stories, through her eyes, that marvelous connection is being made. To see the words, to feel the emotions, is to finally accept the beauty within animals that can change our own lives.

Her goal is simply this—to make the world a better place for all living creatures.

Jerry Finch<br>
Habitat for Horses<br>
A Nonprofit Growth and Learning Center<br>
Hitchcock, Texas<br>
http://www.habitatforhorses.org/

# *Introduction*

The publisher told me I should write something short but exciting for those skimming the beginning of the book. It's supposed to make someone want to run right out and buy the book, take it home, and devour it in a single setting. I asked if I should list my favorite meal to make them hungry, but was told that was not appropriate.

Not appropriate! How much of my life has been bound by those words. Thank goodness, I'm old enough that my mother no longer creeps out of my mouth. My grandmother does, instead. My mother is a true lady, and dearly appreciated by me, but my Nana was a woman of immense wisdom, great humor, and a true original. With my laying claim to her philosophy pushing me, I get to be almost eccentric in my passion for my animals. What a relief! Who said growing old was hard to do?

My personal philosophy is to present my beloved animals in all their glory and uniqueness. This collection and the stories within it were created to share that joy in the existence of others and experience their wonder through my words. If I touch even one other person I have succeeded in that endeavor. Before I discard my "serious" hat and resume the light-hearted storyteller role, let me share with you some words I came by lately, written by Henry Beston, in his *The Outermost House*.

"We need another and a wiser and perhaps more mystical concept of animals.... We patronize them for their incompleteness, for their tragic fate of having taken form so far below ourselves. And therein we err, and greatly err. For the animal shall not be measured by man. In a world older and more complete than ours, they move finished and complete, gifted with extensions of the senses we have lost or never attained, living by voices we shall never hear. They are not underlings, they are other nations, caught with ourselves in the net of life and time, fellow travelers through the splendor of God's plan."

Like good country music, Henry "tells it how it is." Consider yourself part of my family, grab a cup of coffee, drag a hay bale over, take a cookie, and let's just enjoy some barn chat.

# *In the Beginning…*

When I came down here to Texas from up North, I brought a dream with me. It was engraved on my heart, embodied in the horses that came with me—a dream of peaceful plenty for my babies, of winters without freezing rain, ice, and frozen water. We would have a small sanctuary, where we could spend days in quiet enjoyment of green fields by still waters. I was so tired; I just wanted to work this new job and take it easy. I had fought the good fight and was ready to rest. It was someone else's turn to take up the torch; I was too weak to carry it anymore.

Hitchcock attracted me because of the ample land, rural nature, and the presence of a large equine rescue facility. I would not be faced with being the only place for miles that took in discards, horses in need. Someone else was fighting for the horses, and I could cheer them on from a safe distance. Since my herd was paired/grouped except for one elderly palomino mare, I was looking for another horse, an elderly gelding that would be a companion for my TGO (The Golden One) and could slip over to the Habitat For Horses and pick one at my leisure. I was going to love living here—maybe volunteer a bit again but only from a safe distance. This was going to be the life; I still smile at my naiveté.

I called Habitat For Horses and made arrangements with Jerry Finch to come over and see the place after explaining my need. My husband and I went over on a Saturday afternoon and faced a huge herd of horses, some old, some young, bays, chestnuts, Appaloosas, and grays. Jerry took the time to show me around and gently talked about each horse as we met it. Each horse had a name, a past, and a future promise. As Jerry talked, something amazing occurred before me. This gentle man's eyes blazed with a will strong enough to burn the very flesh from his body. The soul that is Jerry is so large, so vibrant, mere skin cannot contain it. He overflows into the air around him and infects others with the sense of his presence, his goal, and his dreams. If you never knew the purity that is horse, five minutes in Jerry's company would have you dreaming horse dreams. His words flowed around me, and I felt the past pain of these horses, the present happiness, and the future hope. Somehow I staggered out of there committed to taking six instead of one, and as my husband and I drove away, he commented that it was good to see the spark back in my eyes.

That infection has spread through my being over the last few years, and as I look back and think of the triumphs, the pain, the pleasure of renewed commitment to the essence of horse, all of those memories have Jerry beside me cheering me on. When I have huddled in the mud frantically clutching the feeble discards of a horse that has gone on, it has been Jerry's hands that have lent me the strength to let go and stand up. When I've been so tired my tremors threaten to overwhelm me, Jerry has stood there shaking his fist into the air and proclaiming, "Enough! Here we draw the line. No more!" and mercifully, sometimes it's worked. I used to look at the times it didn't, but he remembers the times it did. He taught me to stop looking at the half-empty and start looking at the half-full. My husband claims that being able to work with Jerry has dropped years off our lives and maybe if we could bottle the essence of that, we would make a fortune to be donated to the Habitat For Horses.

In this state, this county, and this town, there are horses that are now safe, that are becoming rotund, with convex rather than concave sides. In this time, there are horses that know peace and plenty rather than want and despair. At this place in space and eternity, there is a bright beacon shining through the darkness of the world. There is a veritable vortex of movement in the air, a sense of presence that mutters from deep in our unconsciousness. All is centered and framed within that burning will I met that day and the man who exudes it, Jerry Finch.

Jerry, you inspire us to go that extra step, look for more information, and promise one more horse that it will be safe. Without you, I am one small voice, a tiny bit of resistance to the world's apathy, the guardian of fifteen equine, a dreamer of dreams. With you, I become part of a force to reckon with. I become *we*, and we will move mountains to become the guardians of All. We are the voice of the voiceless, the keepers of the dream. We are the wind that will roar through the halls of justice.

# *Horse Ears, Tails, and Everything in Between*

Now, just hold your horses! (I've always wanted to say that to someone—mainly, because I truly know what it takes to hold a horse that wants to go.) If you bought this book thinking it was full of cute, gentle tales about wonderful, ribbon-winning horses, you'd better take it back. My horses, although very loving, loyal, and gentle creatures are not mane-and tail-flowing dream creations. They are closer to being the discards of today's throwaway society, tattered and tossed by the storms of life. I named my place The Last Refuge for two reasons: one public, one private. The public one is that this sanctuary provides a safe place for elderly and special-needs equines to dream of days of glory in shade-dappled pastures next to a deep, cool pond. They come here thin, downtrodden, dispirited, and quiet. In the space of a moment, they are transformed into individual personalities with quirks, humor, pathos, and a decisive set of likes and dislikes. (There! That sounds so much better than saying, "They have whims and whimsies.")

Ever since I was a young child, horses have marched through my dreams. First, as pretend horses, then as stable rentals, a leased horse, and finally, I met and fell in love with a swaybacked, elderly carriage horse that I paid $25 for when I was a young teenager. To me, he embodied the essence of Horse. His stumbling steps were transformed in my vision to glides of grace and elegance. Rather than perceiving his belly-dragging shamble, I saw poetry. His elderly sunken eyes spoke love and faith to me as I sat mute and listened to the music of his existence. He followed after me, gladly entering into my world of pretend and hope. When he passed on, he left a legacy deeply embedded in my soul. I had met Horse—and I was his forever. That is the source of many of the stories in this book, the wonderment of Horse.

What? I didn't share the private reason for the name of the sanctuary with you? Okay, let me see if I can explain it and still keep half my audience. When I was a child, at one of the many schools I attended, while horse dreams drifted through my consciousness, we had to commit to memory a quote each week. We were given latitude on what to memorize, but if we did not have a quote ready for Monday morning, we would get a zero for that day. I admit to being scatterbrained at the time (and yes, sometimes that trait still lingers), and I got sidetracked easily. One Monday morning, I had no memorized quote ready and I was called on to recite. I stood and declaimed, "The last refuge in an uncaring world is a sense of humor." After ascribing it to the thirteenth-century philosopher and mathematician Roger Bacon, I sat down, bowed my head, and waited for retribution from the heavens above. My teacher complimented me on my quote and went on to the next student. I bore the internal shame of my deception until the break, and then I crawled up to the teacher's desk and confessed my turpitude. She laughed and told me that if Roger Bacon hadn't said it, he should have. I got a zero for the homework memorization and 100 % for the original creation. It has turned into one of my favorite quotes, and I'm sure Roger Bacon would appreciate it if he could hear me, to this day, crediting him with helping create the name of my sanctuary.

# Westward How?

Consulting used to be easy. Work a few months here, a year there. There was always another assignment right down the road, and I didn't need to travel far from my home in the beautiful green hills of Connecticut. As the 1990s headed toward the 2000s, however, a change occurred in my world. Insurance companies combined with each other and processing centers moved south and west. With the slow migration westward, Connecticut was being quietly drained of jobs in my chosen field. To consult meant becoming a road warrior and each new assignment took me farther from home and my heartstrings. I was not home enough to actively participate in animal rescue work and my farm slid into the quietness of a sanctuary for the few horses left on it. My husband faced each winter with less spirit, and trips home for the weekends never left enough time for us to enjoy ourselves. I could only look forward to riding the red-eye home, catching up on chores, and traveling the weary miles back to wherever I was currently stationed. We talked about my finding a job that kept me home, and he agreed to move wherever that might be.

At the time, I was a technology consultant, a Jack-of-all-trades technical translator, down here in Texas, and I mentioned my quandary to my clients. Within a week, they came back with an offer for full time employment. I was grateful and appreciative of the incredible culture and people that represented the company, and I took the proffered employment packet with humble thanks. The company even offered to relocate my family, pets, and horses as part of the package. Well! So much for the fine art of negotiation. In one rapid paragraph, they had offered all I could ever have asked for. I called my husband and asked, "So, how about Texas?" I'm sure the fact he was dealing with the third major ice storm of the season and had not seen the ground bare of snow in six weeks had nothing substantial to do with his quick agreement, but it might have had a peripheral effect.

My husband (other than for six weeks as a small boy) had never lived more than thirty miles away from where he was born, and, like a true swamp Yankee, he had no notion about the world outside of New England. What he knew about Texas was based on old John Wayne movies and a glorified vision of cowboys, flavored by the television show *Dallas*. I'm also convinced he had no concept of just how far away Texas was from Connecticut. He was habituated to being able to travel through seven states in a day and still have time to sightsee before dinner. A long trip was to Boston and back, plus moving, meant loading everything in a U-Haul, as well as a couple of trips with the stock trailer to move the horses. But he was convinced that being away from winter and having me home every evening was worth the small amount of trouble a move would be. He'd made his decision, and that was that in his mind. I had been raised in a military family, moved many times, and knew better, but I just smiled and kept my silence.

Our farm in Connecticut was a typical New England set-up—old house, new barn, water by well, and heat by wood stove. For much of the year, wealth was measured by the height of the woodpile and the depth of the stack of hay. Green was fleeting, but it was emerald rich for the few short months it graced the fields and trees. Autumn lavished rich splendor as it borrowed russets and gold from the sunset. The town we resided near had 3500 residents—if you counted the dogs, and everyone had a dog or two. Visits to the grocery store and pizza shop were punctuated by vocalized greetings from the canine front-seat passengers of the cars in the parking lot. We talked about going "down to the city" as if it were a thousand miles away rather than the steeply winding traverse of foothills and valleys that made up the bulk of the twenty-mile trip. Ice-slick, narrow country roads, bounded by unforgiving stone fences, had long ago taught rural Connecticut residents caution in driving, and a reasonable speed was 35 mph in the clear areas.

Hitchcock, Texas, is also a small town, with one grocery store; one could say the two locations have some similarity. Well, they're similar except Hitchcock's hills are the mounds next to the drainage ditches, and ice comes in glasses, not on the ground. The new farm was a gleam in my eyes; I had purchased 25 acres of raw land and was proposing to build on it. I had the idealistic viewpoint that we could live in a mobile home while we cleared the land and built the house and barn. Lots of people got their farms started that way. I'm not sure where those lots of people got started, but I bet it wasn't in Hitchcock. I should have realized I was in trouble when a small joke about starting out as PWTT (poor white trailer trash) created a raised eyebrow and the comment, "We don't want any more trailers moving into Hitchcock" and a "Here's the twenty-five forms you need to have filled out, notarized, signed by all your neighbors within half a mile, and then we'll talk about whether you can have that trailer temporarily on the property or not." All right, so I had the raw (translated as fenceless, thorn-covered, boggy, with mounds of scrap metal in back) land; there was plenty of time to fix it up before my husband came down. It would take forever to sell the place in Connecticut. Two weeks later, an offer for the farm came in with no contingencies—and oh, could they close in a month?

I will spare you the tale of the next few weeks because, towards the end, I was tossing more than packing, and I was still trying to map out how to drive 1400 miles with three dogs and two cats on a route that would take me past a dog park on a just-in-time basis. There was no way we were going to be able to get a motel room with the four-legged passengers, so it was decided to sell my Jeep, ship the truck, and rent a passenger van large enough so that everyone had their own seat. Somehow, between getting the horses loaded into the commercial hauler; clearing the house into the moving van; losing the fight over whether they loaded the snow plow—just in case; rounding up the dogs and cats for the fifth time; doing the final walk-through of the farm; handing the keys over; picking up the huge passenger van; loading it and heading down the road, I forgot to visit the ladies room, so our first stop was a mile from home instead of two hundred. My husband took the opportunity to slide over from the driver's chair to the passenger's chair, and he was sound asleep when I got back in. He slept most of the next thousand miles, rousing only for meals and dog walk breaks. He woke up the last few hours but was too excited by all the new scenery to consider driving. As we pulled into Hitchcock, he commented on how fast the trip had taken, and he brightly observed that I looked a little pale. I contemplated the image of him roasting over a slow fire for a moment, but the insurance wouldn't pay off—so he still lives.

Although the move down here has been good in many ways, it has been an education for him. He did not see the function or use of the large drainage ditches that border the roads until the first drenching rain hit, and we faced firsthand the end results of fifteen inches of rain in eight hours. Fortunately, it occurred while I was still negotiating with my husband over the large stock tank (everywhere but Texas, it would be called a pond) I wanted to dig and use the dirt to build a small platform for the house and barn. After the rain, he decided I wanted too small a tank, so we doubled its size. We have the first real hill in Hitchcock, and our house and barn perch on it. It makes a great view, and my stock tank is eighteen feet deep and an acre across. So flood or drought, we should be safe. The first winter, he watched the temperatures plummet in New England on the Weather Channel, looked outside at the sixty-degree days and smiled. The second winter, he finally put the snowplow away in the barn. I'm figuring that next winter, he will start complaining that it's chilly here if it drops to seventy. I'll know he's a real Texan then.

The horses have discovered the joys of year-round grass and, after the neighbor's bull strolled though the kitchen door, I did get busy and finish the fencing. Somehow, my three dogs became five (in the city, people have to go buy a dog; in the country, people drive by and drop them in your yard for free), and I've acquired a flock of pigeons, some ducks, eighteen bee hives, many cats, three mules, and a dozen or so more horses. Someone down here is sure generous with leaving animals in my yard. It must be that open Texas hospitality I've heard so much about.

# GoWyeth

The story of GoWyeth begins when I still lived up north and was first struggling to find a way to get selling-to-slaughter stopped. It is a story reconstructed based on a tattoo, a lot of legwork, and some guesses. More than that it, is the story of the pain that drives me.

GoWyeth was a large, gray standard-bred stallion who faced the meat man twice, and he is my horse for all times. For me, his story is one of courage and heart; it embodies all that means *horse*. I always thought of him as my southern gentleman because of his manners and his snowy-white "ice cream" suit. He was a trotter, born to race, and in his youth he dedicated his great heart and mile-covering massive trot to winning many races and pumping money and fame into the hands of his owner and trainer. For a few brief years, he was the prize of their racing stable. But, like all racehorses, he got older and his racing days were over.

They brought him home off the road, and he was used as a stud for awhile, but none of his offspring had his fire, his heart. GoWyeth was put into a back pasture to retire and become forgotten. No more carrots, kisses, and caresses. He sighed and looked toward the house where his owner used to come from, and he waited for visits that never came. His owner had suffered a stroke and gone into a nursing home, and the son of a cousin took over operation of the farm. He decided to streamline the operation and put some of the "worthless" horses up for sale. A man towing several sharp-faced kids showed up and bought the old horse and several others for his kids. GoWyeth was loaded onto their stock trailer and hauled away. Like an old car, he was sold "as is," with no warranties or promises on either side. The farm's new manager went back inside, marked a few hundred dollars in the asset column of the books, and wrote off four useless horses. He had shown a profit and was pleased.

GoWyeth's new owners, who had promised to "take care of him all his life," as they loaded him into the over-crowded trailer, headed north where they promptly dumped him out and sold him at auction to a hack stable in Massachusetts. The stable found out he could be pummeled and pounded on all day by a conglomeration of non-riders yet still be willing to do all they wanted. GoWyeth carried "thumpers," "side pounders," "back bouncers," and "run them till they droppers" with dignity and heart. Of course, by the end of the day, his nose bled and his feet hurt but he still carried his head high. And so the years went—he worked spring, summer, and fall—and then he scrounged forage by eating bark off of trees in the winter. At a rental price of $30 an hour, he earned his keep.

Then came the day the humane society visited the hack stable and noticed GoWyeth had cancer. Melanoma was growing around his rectum and between his legs. The humane society officer felt this was not a good image to present to the world on a hack horse and told the stable owner to put him down. GoWyeth had served well and was tired. He almost felt relief when he was loaded into the van with the other "rejected" horses. But putting a horse down costs money, and the stable owner didn't want to waste that kind of money on old, used-up horses, so instead of heading to the vet's office, GoWyeth and the others were off to an auction house. This particular auction sold horses for meat, as well as other purposes, so it appeared that GoWyeth's fate was sealed and he would go by the pound on the "European Tour."

Life is not so simple, however. The night GoWyeth was led out into the auction ring, the meat men noticed he was old, tattered, and worn down and started joke-bidding for his life at $25. In an ironic gesture of classic proportions, a very inebriated hack stable owner from Connecticut was also bidding. It was dark, he was drunk, and he didn't see the melanoma. He saw only a cheap horse, so he bid and bought GoWyeth for the princely sum of $350. The next day, the hung-over stable owner was outraged at his "bargain." His new horse was worthless, a bag of bones, thin from a lean winter and tired, so very tired. But bought he was, so the stable owner took him home to work off his "debt." He soon found that, bag of bones or not, GoWyeth would carry his load. For 14 to 16 hours a day, seven days a week, GoWyeth hacked and stumbled his way through life. His eyes dimmed, and as the summer wore on, he rarely lifted his head to look at the world. Bowed and silent, he did his job. He more than earned back his cost, but still he trudged, often carrying doubles. His frame, at least, was large enough to carry a man and a child—if one didn't look at his lack of flesh.

Then came the height of summer in Connecticut, and temperatures soared into the 90s. The hack line continued marching over the hills into a state park each day. Ironically, fate was repeating itself, for the Connecticut humane officer was now yelling about this horse. People would see him and complain, and the humane officer was saying, "Take care of that horse now," but GoWyeth was a guaranteed ride, so hack he did. The stable owner would promise grandly to feed him more, take him off the line, and after the humane officer left, he would put GoWyeth back on line. This game went on until the day he collapsed from the heat and the weight of his rider in the park. The trail leader was angry and pulled at GoWyeth to get up, but GoWyeth lay feeble and down. Not even his great heart could get him up off the ground to carry his load another step. Finally he staggered to his feet and stood head down, waiting for the end. He was being walked back to the barn down the road when he fell again at the front of my property.

I heard the commotion down the drive; my dog was screaming his alert cry, and my horses were frantic. I went down to the road and faced chaos and a melee of confusion. A broken, yellowed horse was trying to climb off bloody, frayed knees to his feet. A tattered saddle was dangling under his belly. GoWyeth was foaming and bleeding from his nose, broken-footed, shaking and swaying. The stable owner drove up in a battered Ford with a pony trailer attached and attempted to load him in. I heard auction, saw pain, and reacted instinctively. I bought him on the spot for the meat price (I told the owner it saved him the cost of towing him to the meat market) and coaxed him up my driveway. I started hosing him and called my vet to come immediately—I had an emergency. The vet raced over, thinking one of my others was hurt, saw my new horse and almost dropped his teeth. I had bought a ghost, an animated skeleton, and a whisper of what hell would look like. Where the blanket and saddle had rubbed his poor bony back were cratered sores big enough to put a fist in, and his feet bled when he walked. I disappeared into the pool of pain in his eyes and shook uncontrollably. But the cold hosing revived him and, behind the pain, his eyes were kind, so instead of putting him down immediately, we decided to give him a few weeks of kindness to savor before allowing him the sleep he had earned.

The next few weeks gave GoWyeth strength for a few more weeks, and he began to put weight on. His eyes brightened, his voice came back, his neck arched again, and there before me was a magnificent white stallion. The humane society officer came to see him after confronting the hack stable owner about where the "cancer horse" was and didn't recognize GoWyeth. It's funny what a little food and love will do. For too short a space of time, GoWyeth was my best friend. We would talk for hours as I groomed him and he nuzzled me. He used to follow me around like a puppy, and I gladly baby-sat all that came after him. We had a glorious year and a half together before the cancer spread to his intestines, and my vet said it was time. Our last night together, his eyes were dim but he lifted his head and nickered to me when I spoke to him. I dissolved into a puddle of misery afterwards, unable to see past the loss. My vet put his arm on my shoulder and said the kindest thing he could have. He told me I had given GoWyeth "all the time that he had." That gentle soul is in a green meadow somewhere near the Rainbow Bridge, with all the mares and their babies around him, and I know his neck is arched and his nickers warm and fragrant with welcome to each day. He was my first "meat purchase," and sometimes when I sit up at night with a new, sick one, I can hear GoWyeth's voice in the distance of my soul, encouraging and heartening me. I have promised his memory to give all the horses all the time that they have, to allow none to have their lives cut short and blown out their nostrils in pools of their own blood.

# Cindy Lou, Where Are You?

Every time Jerry invites me out to Habitat because he "wants to show me something," I know he is not offering to sit me by the lake and let me gaze at the sunset.

"Show me something" has ranged from a seriously ill donkey (Duke, my lawn ornament, my porch-hanging-out wonder), to a frozen-kneed, gap-toothed old quarter horse (Buster Brown; he's my clown), to a myriad of other "Get the trailer out, I'm coming home, Maude" wonders that rapidly merge into The Last Refuge's herd and my heart. On a particularly bad afternoon at work, hung off the tail of the fifth Monday of a week, the phone rang.

"Stop by at the ranch, Carol. I have something to show you."

"I'm not bringing any more home for awhile, Jerry. I still have two new ones in the front yard and they are not stable enough yet to move to the back fields."

Jerry laughed, agreed, and said he'd see me in half an hour or so. He slid that hook in so deftly I never felt it settle into my cheek.

I car pool to work with a chocolate-box beauty named Cindy, and, for those not familiar with that term, "chocolate-box beauties" are people not only fair to look at but are also chock full of sweetness, generosity, and occasionally a bit nutty. Cindy has china doll features, wonderful twinkling eyes, and a rosebud complexion surmounted by gilded locks. It's a comedic tragedy that I could never play Rose Red to her Snow White since we are inseparable "sisters in spirit." She "pays for the dressing," as my grandmother used to say, and I choose clothes based on durability, stain resistance, and ease of movement. Suffice to say, people at work occasionally mention gently that they've seen me in a dress only once in two years and that was for a fundraiser for the United Way. I feel since people are willing to donate to charity to see me fettered in a dress, why dissipate that wonder by repeating it too often?

The afternoon in question sank slowly into a morass of untangled skeins of code rewritten, patted-into-place logic, and completed batches of reports "that *have* to be done tonight, Carol." Firmly ignoring the far-off calls of an incipient migraine, I sulked downstairs to Cindy's office and grumped about Jerry wanting to show me something. Cindy grinned and admitted he had called her, as well.

Wrapped with laptop and other incidentals in a modern version of Bob Morley's chains, I trailed behind her elegant, high-heeled stroll to the elevator bank.

Once outside, I clambered into the truck, she gently slid in, and we were off. Somehow, my soft sigh of relief, emitted as the causeway carried us off the island toward home, translated into the winds of change blowing us towards the Habitat ranch rather than my own. Cindy assures me it was that or the hook in my cheek that reeled me in.

Something deposited us in the driveway where Jerry stood waiting, unholy glee in his eyes. Something propelled my weak, weary frame out of the truck and through the gate, stopping in front of a small intake paddock. Cindy and I stood next to Jerry, looking in at an ancient chestnut, white-blanket Appaloosa and a young rose-colored mare.

I stubbornly waited for Jerry to talk, he looked slyly at me, and we were at a standstill. Neither one of us was going to commit to going first on the discussion of why these two needed to come to The Last Refuge. The hook had now been firmly set in my cheek and the line was growing taut, but I played dead on the end of the string and waited to see if he would give up.

There is a sound I make when I'm ready to capitulate—a soft, low croon that rises from the depths of my heart and eases past my tightened throat and out parted lips. Jerry generally waits for that signal, then reels me in. With disbelief, I heard the crooning and turned to see Cindy staring in awe at the horses. Cindy has always admired my herd from the safety of the path on the other side of the fence.

Cindy, she of the divine proportions, sleekly groomed manner, and perfect hair, was beaming love and emitting an almost greedy desire at two horses. I was going to enjoy watching her capitulate to the wonders of horses and their "by-products." Jerry (looking straight ahead) softly started talking about the elderly Appaloosa gelding, Chief, and how he was bonded only to the mare, Red. He deftly fished, dropping bait about how old Chief was and no one wanted to adopt him. Only offers for Red came in.

Twitching the pole slightly, he continued about how separating them would break Chief's heart. Chief would not eat without Red, and there was no adopter to take them as a pair. Tugging the line to set the hook, he finished up by saying Habitat was again overloaded, and he either had to separate these two and adopt out Red singly, or perhaps I might find room for both.

The sound of crooning filled the air, and Jerry turned to face us in triumph. The light of victory was in his eyes as he gazed at my closed lips and dropped his jaw. I might have been giggling silently but the croon was not originating from me. Flipping his head sideways, he saw my elegant friend singing from her heart to the two horses. Looking back at me, he cocked his head, and I nodded assent. He might have gone fishing for Carol but he had reeled in Cindy.

The two horses came to stay at The Last Refuge the next day. I've renamed Red Cindy Lou, and she and Chief are an inseparable pair, wandering the pasture in a duet of love. They are fast friends, and shadow each other in equine illustration of Cindy's and my friendship. Just as Chief has gained youth from Cindy Lou, she is learning patience from him. Friendships do that. The bond melds two into one, and each draws from the other. Old married couples and long-established friends start to look a bit alike. Cindy's Mike and my Richard always hoped we would do the same. I believe, however, neither anticipated Cindy's learning to love horses, get muddy, and let the wind flow through her hair as part of that mutual exchange. I think the look becomes her and, in the process of teaching her the values of solid, no-nonsense dressing, she has taught me to enjoy shopping. However, the story of how a "go in, get what you need, leave in under fifteen minutes" person learned to shop can wait for another day. There are noses to kiss outside, and Cindy is here with a load of carrots to take into the back field across the mud-filled drainage ditch.

# *Viewing Responsibility through Rose-Colored Glasses*

In *The Little Prince,* Antoine de Saint-Exupéry has created a parable of awakening enlightenment. The little prince, struggling to keep a rose safe from the sheep, meets a fox, who asks whether he has tamed his rose.

"What does that mean—tame?" queries the little prince.

The fox replies, "It is an act too often neglected. It means to establish ties.... One only understands the things that one tames. You are responsible, forever, for what you have tamed. You are responsible for your rose."

I have a Rose whom I have tamed, and I am responsible for her. Her full name is Lady Sterling Rose, and I purchased her for 85 cents a pound from a "killer-buyer" who was waiting outside a slaughterhouse to deliver his trailer load of dozens of horses. Rose's only flaw was that she had too few spots for her breed standard. For want of a few black hairs, she was auctioned off in Minnesota and hauled thousands of miles to a slaughter plant, a place that stuns, bleeds, and carves up hundreds of horses daily.

As I stood at the edge of the holding pen, the horses' screams filled my ears as piercingly as the scent of blood permeated my nostrils. If I hadn't chanced upon the killer-buyer and his offer of a horse in exchange for "eatin' money," Rose would have ended up on a dinner table in France, Italy, Belgium, or Japan. Her glorious eyes would not have viewed another sunset. The nicker she greets me with would have been stilled forever. At eighteen months, she would have become one more statistic—there were 42,312 of them in the U.S. last year—hidden behind the slaughterhouse walls.

Few people know that horses are slaughtered in the U.S. to please palates abroad. Fewer still have gained access to the plants to see the slaughtering firsthand. One such witness is Christopher J. Heyde, a policy analyst for The Society for Animal Protective Legislation. "Once in the hands of the killer-buyers, horses are subjected to unimaginable cruelty and suffering," he explains. "They receive little or no water or food during transport. At the slaughterhouse, their suffering continues. Poorly trained, callous workers beat horses indiscriminately with thick, fiberglass rods. Often because of improper and inadequate efforts to render them insensitive to pain prior to slaughter, horses may be dismembered while still conscious."

For thousands of years, mankind has treated horses as partners in work and companions in play. In return, horses have offered loyalty and love, strength and speed. We humans and our horses have tamed each other. But when it comes to responsibility, it's not a two-way street. They are not responsible for us—or for what we do to them. We alone are responsible for them—and to them. It is our sacred obligation to uphold the trust that horses have placed in us.

Somehow, supporters of horse slaughter have missed that point. They see nothing wrong with violating the unwritten covenant that was established generations ago. As long as there's a dollar to be made, advocates of slaughter will continue to resist the efforts of humanitarians to ban it. Thus, the only way to end the execution of American horses is to pass a federal law. That is why Rep. John Sweeney (R-NY) and Rep. John Spratt (D-SC) introduced HR 857, the American Horse Slaughter Prevention Act, in February 2003. A Senate version of the bill is waiting to be introduced at any time.

My own state, Texas, is home to the last two horse slaughterhouses in the U.S. The irony is that we are one of the few states with a law prohibiting the practice. When the Texas Attorney General attempted to uphold that 54-year-old law last year, the slaughter plants' foreign owners immediately filed an injunction in federal court. Then they lobbied for a bill in the state legislature that would legalize their operations (see "Horse-Meat Sales Stir Texas Controversy," *Christian Science Monitor*, April 28, 2003). They didn't count on the overwhelming grassroots opposition. Calls, letters, faxes and e-mails from more than a million horse lovers around the country and from as far away as Spain forced the Austin politicians to let the bill die.

In the meantime, the slaughterhouses are still in business, pending a ruling on their request for a permanent injunction from the federal judge. Every day, approximately 150 young, healthy, agile—and, yes, tame—horses are forced into the kill chutes, knocked unconscious, hung upside down by a chain on a rear leg, and slit at the throat (sometimes still conscious). Why are such perfectly good horses killed? Because no one wants to eat old, stringy ones—to paraphrase a French butcher. And why are U.S. horses in the most demand? Because Americans, for the most part, feed their horses the best.

"You are responsible, forever, for what you have tamed," said the fox to the little prince. That responsibility does not end when we turn a blind eye and allow our horses to be destroyed. We have tamed our horses and named them Rose.

Until HR 857 becomes law, we are viewing responsibility for what we have tamed behind a blindfold instead of through glorious Rose-colored glasses.

# *Short Tails*

I've never been able to pinpoint exactly when a corollary becomes a stated fact, but somehow things we think we know get proven over and over again until they're just plain accepted as being fact rather than theory. Sometimes they are old wives' tales or Internet scare stories, urban legends for a new age; I've been known to refer to them as truisms. I'm sure that sometimes they are even true facts, such as a white horse plus new grass makes a green horse (and the closer it is to show time, the greener the result). Certainly horse-keeping people tend to collect and use a lot of these truisms.

One truism flapping around my unconscious belief system is that all rescued horses come with short tails. It's as if they had been left in a herd of foals and had them chewed on. Foals, one may ask? Just as toddlers delight in grabbing their mother's hair and swinging from it, foals suck and chew on the nearest thing they can grab. That always seems to be the longest, proudest tails in the herd. After they've reduced their mother's tail to a few spindly strands of neck-stretched length, they graduate to whatever horses in the herd are dumb enough to believe that "I'm a baby face" means the foal is harmless. Here comes this cute, big-eyed wonder that clacks his teeth and grins, the hapless older horse nuzzles it, turns its back, and all at once the cute little foal mouth turns into an industrial-sized vacuum and sucks half the length of the poor horse's tail off. In a good afternoon, an active foal can reduce the collective tail length of a herd by an easy twenty feet. Within the short space of a week, most of the herd looks as if their tails were bobbed, and the foal just grins at its next chosen snack.

Every newly rescued horse I've been around either has no tail left, or if there is one, it's so fouled up that the only way to get all the birds' nests out of it is to cut it. Either way, after the first twenty-four hours of being at the rescue facility, they all seem to end up with stubby little promises of tails. Sometimes even the forelocks fall victim to the same "liberation from servitude" to burrs, brambles, and bushes that cast-off hunks of tail bear mute testimony to. The tattered, clean remnants of flowing tresses are left to regain strength and growth again. This truism can be applied as the definitive clock for length of time in rescue—that is, how far have the tail and mane grown back? If it's three inches, the horse needs more rehab. Six inches—time to start looking for a new home. A foot—probably in their forever home, for the new flock of vultures (er, foals) has not been born yet.

Because I spend so much time and effort working with rescues, however, I tend to forget that "normal" horses have tails and flowing manes, sweeping waves of glorious hair. So when I come across a horse abundantly endowed with tresses that flow unfettered toward the ground, I am at a loss for a minute. I look around furtively and then tentatively stroke the hair to actually feel the reality of my vision. Horses really do have parts of them that can float in the wind, unencumbered by half the forest primeval.

# *New Names Are the Stepping Stones to the Future*

There have been quite a few human societies in which the practice of providing new names to mark turning points in one's life was routinely practiced. A name was given to a child at birth; then the child earned more descriptive names as it grew up. Many of the Native American tribes practiced this custom, and I've always thought it was wonderful to be able to earn one's name by one's behavior.

Most of my "babies" come here because of a horrible existence. They have faced pain, suffering, neglect, and deprivation. The names they arrive with are evocative of that past. Many of them cringe when called by those names. For this reason, they are offered a change in identity to go along with their new lives. It's always a challenge to provide an acceptable name for each one, and a lot of deliberation goes into the naming ritual.

Everyone that comes in starts off as "Sweetie." It's a good sound and promises softness, caring, and acceptance. Slowly, the names migrate to "Baby," "Honey," or "Doll." These too are temporary titles that mark the stages of transition from scared to spoiled. Somewhere in that sequence comes a time, individual to each horse, when a new name settles in and becomes accepted. When that occurs, the naming ritual takes place. We have a nameplate carved with the new name, and it is ceremoniously put up on the stable office wall to commemorate our newest named. We have quite a wall full of them now, but they are never removed. I can sit in the office and look at them and remember.

I remember Charger. He won his name by turning from a shy, withdrawn horse into one full of the exuberance of life. He used to charge across the field, flinging his heels to the sky and bugling with joy in the spring.

I remember The Beef Master. He was a scrawny, malnourished 590-pound bag of bones when he arrived. He left here a massive 1400-pound beefy (as wide as he was tall) eating machine.

I remember Mouser. She won this appellation the day she reached into her hay bin, discovered a mouse, and came through the stall door (leaving it on the floor in her wake), screaming in terror. From then on, she would dump all the hay out and shake it with vigor, looking out for any stray mice before she condescended to eat.

I remember Boots. Contrary to what you might suppose, he didn't have white stockings (we never seem to give obvious names to our brood). Boots had a habit of grabbing my Wellingtons and flinging them out into the field. He'd then charge after them, kick as hard as he could, then pounce, grab, shake, and fling them all over again. I finally donated one pair to his exclusive use as he had such a good time with them. In fact, he took them with him to his new home, and the last I heard, he was still playing with them.

I remember Flag. He was a strawberry roan with a white blaze down his face. His name derived from his love of blueberries. He'd cram his head through the fence rails and eat the forbidden blueberries off my bushes with great relish and massive blue staining around his lips. The sight of that red, white, and blue face sent me into gales of laughter, shouting he looked just like a flag. The name stuck (as did the blue coloring, I'm afraid).

Yes, as I sit in the office and drink coffee, the names on the wall call me and fill me with memories. There is a common thread to my remembrances; a golden glow surrounds each name. These plaques symbolize new beginnings—and new beginnings cry out for new names. New names are stepping stones to a new life, and wouldn't we all like to be able to do that at one point or another in our own lives?

# Tall Ears—the Coming of the IRS Drug Mules

✦

*(Official Version, according to Press Releases)*

When Special Agent Dan Pieschel of the Criminal Investigations Unit of the IRS was faced with liquidating the seized proceeds from a drug dealer's operations, he quickly realized that many of the hundreds of thousands of dollars in assets came on four legs. Although, as Agent Pieschel plaintively stated, the IRS usually does not seize anything that eats while the leaders of the drug ring are behind bars. Thus, the horses, mules, and cattle were faced with deprivation and neglect. Usually the only victim in a criminal case brought by the IRS is the U.S. government. However, these defendants from a small town in central Kentucky used the proceeds from their illegal drug business to purchase and raise over 150 registered Tennessee Walkers, Percheron drafts, Belgian drafts, horses and mules. By the time the defendants admitted their guilt and agreed to give their livestock to the IRS, the new owners (IRS) discovered they had live victims that needed immediate attention.

The defendants, who were unable to care for the animals after their arrests, turned them over to the IRS-Criminal Investigation agents who began the arduous, two-months task of bringing the horses and mules back to good health. One mare had already given birth to a healthy mule, and many more foals were on the way. Agent Pieschel (who admitted to being allergic to anything with fur) was committed to the daunting task of developing a plan to market and sell the animals. The United States Department of the Treasury contracted with EG&G Technical Services of Gaithersburg, Maryland, to manage custody, storage, and disposal of the Treasury's seized property. EG&G immediately made arrangements to have the animals moved and maintained on other farms. However, the IRS needed to sell them as soon as possible to protect the animals and the government's interest.

"These horses, even the registered, purebred show horses, need a second chance," said Fred Borakove, IRS-Criminal Investigation Special Agent in Charge, Louisville Field Office. "While some of the horses were still being maintained, many more were not properly cared for after the defendants were arrested. Our agency is following an agreement that allows us to provide these animals with appropriate food and care, and bring them to auction to protect the interest of the United States Treasury."

Pieschel has had extensive experience in handling assets such as real property, automobiles, boats, and the like, but livestock was a new challenge for a man raised in the confines of the city. Pieschel discovered that over 150 horses come with far more problems than feeding them. First, he dealt with a public concern by the Humane Society that the animals were not being properly cared for by the government. EG&G Services immediately hired a local veterinarian to verify the condition and care of the horses. "I oversaw all of the medical care of these animals from the day the IRS-Criminal Investigation took custody," said Dr. Ted Cundiff, DVM from Richmond, Kentucky. "The agency took all the appropriate steps to make sure these horses were healthy and fit for auction." The horses were primarily mares, many of which were pregnant and ready to foal.

The traditional way of selling seized assets is at public auction. Pieschel was unaware, but educated by alarmed horse lovers, that if these types of horses are sold at public auction, they would likely be slaughtered, their meat and hides sold. Pieschel stated, "This has been an eye opener for me, I never knew all the uses for horse meat." To satisfy this concern, Pieschel reached an agreement with a group of rescues that any horse that did not bring enough at auction to cover the IRS's expenses would be offered for sale to the rescues, which would find homes for the animals.

The Last Refuge, an equine sanctuary in Hitchcock, Texas, ended up purchasing two of the mule babies from the IRS. Dr. Cundiff provided health certificates free of charge for the babies. The auction manager, Jim Dause, joined in the benevolent aura that was surrounding the sale of these once-prized horses and found transportation for two young mules to Texas. Dause knew a goat transporter who had room on a load going to Texas, so Leonard Arlington transported the baby mules to Lometa, Texas. Jerry Finch from Habitat For Horses and Carol Chapman from The Last Refuge made the 750-mile round trip from Hitchcock to Lometa to bring the babies home. "When the babies first arrived they were very skittish, had not been handled much and understandably missed their mothers," said Carol Chapman. "However, an elderly mare we have has taken them under her wing, and they are doing fine here." The mare, a thirty-year-old palomino, has taken her new duties as babysitter very seriously and does not seem to hold the babies' long ears against them. "The IRS went above and beyond to save these babies when their mothers were starving. In honor of that, I have named the older baby "Dan-A-Mule," after the agent who saved them," Chapman said.

The sale took place March 29, 2003, at Richmond Livestock Sales, Richmond, Kentucky. About 3000 people from around the country passed through the show ring during the preview day and sale day. Most of the horses and mules were sold rapidly to buyers aware of their potential. Only a few of them needed to be placed by rescues in caring homes. Fred Borakove, the Special Agent in Charge of the Louisville Field Office, stated, "These horses and mules were victims in this crime and the government makes it a practice to protect victims." Everyone came out a winner in this sale—the buyers at the sale because they were able to get quality animals at discounted prices, the horse sanctuaries because they were able to keep any from ending up in the slaughter pens, and Pieschel and the IRS because they successfully cared for the animals and collected close to $170,000 from the sale.

# The Coming of the IRS Drug Mules

✦

## (Actual Events Uncovered)

Although the facts in the preceding story are true, the flavor has been leeched out of them. There's something sterile about press release requirements that makes all the "good stuff" end up at the bottom of the editor's trash basket. I've taken the liberty of rummaging through it, and here are all the snippets that didn't make the cut.

The drug dealers were not just breeding mules; they were breeding the largest mules in the world. Their mammoth jack mule was kin to the *Guinness Book of World Records*' tallest donkey ever and threw his height, as well as his incredulously large ears, into the mix with fervor. Combine these features with huge draft horse mothers, and you have mules with a capital *M*. The goat transporter called me when he picked up my two babies, Jack and Dan (four and nine months old respectively), and announced loudly, "Lady, these aren't mule babies. These are mountains with ears." And were they ever. The smaller of the two was already taller than my quarter horses, and the larger one was towering over everyone in the herd, and neither "baby" was a year old yet. They were not just mountains with ears; they were Mount Everests with ears.

When I made the arrangements with the goat transporter to haul my babies to Texas, neither he nor I really thought about how big Texas truly is. He told me he was heading for a goat auction in Lometa, not too far from me. I accepted that as being a few hours away. Lometa appeared to be just above Austin. I called my friend Jerry and asked him to go along with me to pick them up—just an easy jaunt up the road. We left early in the morning and headed out, and as we neared Austin, Jerry inquired which way to go next. I unfolded the map and squinted, then told him north. He (in the dangerously quiet tone that men use with women when they are getting aggravated) asked, "How far north?" I held two fingers to the map and proudly proclaimed, "Oh, about three inches of the map more." In even more quiet tones, Jerry stated, "Carol, we are only two inches from home now on that map. How far is this place? And what is its name?"

I quietly squirmed as I said, "I'm not sure how far, but its name is Lometa." I will spare you the ensuing few hours, but it is not true we saw signs that said Oklahoma before we got there.

Lometa is one tiny town. A solitary stoplight with a bank and a convenience store marked the turn. I needed to pay cash to the transporter, so we pulled into the bank parking lot. After looking all around the outside of the bank for an ATM, I opened the door and went in, where I was welcomed by three wooden desks, burly men with boots propped on the desks—and no ATM. After being answered by blank stares when I asked about the existence of an ATM, one of the men condescended to inform me that, of course, there was no ATM at the bank. If I wanted something like that, I'd better go down to the convenience store, where one of "those things" belonged. Unbelieving, but hopeful, I did just that and found the ATM. Cash in hand, we headed down to the goat auction house.

There were goats in pens everywhere, and as I looked for two tiny mule babies, in the distance bugled the unmistakable tones of mule caroling. I looked toward the pen and then up...and up. They certainly were mountains with ears. Jerry (very quietly now) muttered, "Mule babies. Were their mothers giraffes, Carol?" Did I mention the babies were not halter broken, socialized, or in a very good frame of mind about getting onto another trailer, just having come off from one the night before? Perhaps I should just gloss over the next fifteen minutes of coaxing two un-handled mules into the stock trailer. Certainly I will skip over parts of the trip back home—the silent treatment parts, for instance. There was some humor on the highway, however, when people would pull up alongside, glance into the trailer at those ears, and then talk excitedly to each other about whatever they thought we had back there.

Getting home and unloading the mule babies into the quarantine pen was uneventful. Watching them walk up to the pen walls, measure them—and pop over—and then take off down the field to the horse herd was not. Seeing my husband's face as they flat jumped six feet was priceless. As for listening to him and Jerry discuss my lack of common sense—well, let's just mercifully bury that memory, shall we?

The mule babies have settled in and discovered the joys of belonging to a herd. They do look down their noses at the poor stunted ears of the horses, and they quietly snicker even more over my deformed ears. Both Dan and Jack are inordinately proud of those tall, waving stalks of hair and cartilage that they carry so proudly on their heads. They've even started a catch phrase around here, "My hay has ears."

The other morning I went out to greet the herd and count heads, kiss noses, and promise breakfast. There were supposed to be fifteen noses, and I kept coming up with fourteen and recounting and looking. Jack (the baby draft mule) was missing. I called and called and couldn't see him anywhere, so I opened the gate to walk back and start looking.

Half-way down the pasture is a pile of refused hay (wondrous hay, but with fresh grass, they are ignoring it again), and as I moved toward it, the pile shifted, grew legs into the air and stretched and bellowed good morning in the best, loudest, mule bellow I've ever heard. When Jack shifted himself upright, the top of his head was bedecked with a large clump of hay and those two giant, twitching ears went back and forth like windshield wipers clearing rain off a window. Since it is a major affront to laugh at a mule, I almost strangled trying to choke the laughter in.

Jack came up, and the hay that wasn't still on his head had migrated to his back. Being generous, he shook himself like a big dog and shared it with my navy blue suit. One more day of going into work and carrying part of home with me—at least, this was just hay and not recycled stuff. When someone pointed out my suit had hay on it, I choked out, "My hay has ears"—and got the nonsense award of the year for it. But it has made a handy, inane expression at work and been picked up by others to use when there is no answer readily available for something.

I was going to end this episode here, but someone who's reading this demanded to know why I call them IRS Drug Mules. I looked askance at him, and then did the soft sigh, raised eyebrow and other female signals to no avail. I had to explain the pun several times before he groaned and muttered, "Women think they have a sense of humor." I'm hoping I don't actually have to go into the same dance around Drug Mule, IRS Drug Seizure, Drug Runner, Mules Running, and so forth with you. Have a cookie, and it will come to you, I promise.

# Of Goats and Gardens

Once upon a time I had the most beautiful rose garden on my street. My mailbox was always crammed full of plant catalogs, seed offerings, bulb sales, and wish books of all sorts. There was a lot of pride, time, and effort placed in keeping the grounds immaculate. Even the horses appeared to appreciate the beauty and, for the most part, they respected my fences (although what they did to the vegetable garden is another story!).

Then came the arrival of Riley, the year of the goat. My vet had done surgery on a goat that had been savaged by wild dogs. The goat's owner did not want a scarred goat back at his petting zoo, so he brought her over to me as a surprise.

"She'll eat the scrub, the stuff the horses won't touch, and she'll help keep your fields in shape," my vet confidently told me.

"Well, okay," I thought, "this should save me some weed whacker time. What a great idea." My vet and I were in complete agreement about the goat's new chores and responsibilities. Unfortunately, we forgot to check with her for her interpretation of what is edible to a goat.

I admit now to being a neophyte about goats when Riley came, and the goat care book I bought left out a few vital facts. Let me give you a quick run-down on the things Riley did that the book never touched on:

Goats can squeeze under fences that are horse proof. Beautiful white board fences do not a goat keep.

Goats all secretly yearn for the mountains of their ancestors and will happily stand on the hood of any car they can find.

Goats follow some arcane law that states, "Nature abhors a vacuum." For a goat, this means their circumference will expand to accommodate all the goodies they can gobble down. In fact, Riley got so large I accused my vet of giving me a pregnant goat and insisted he come out and check her. The result of the exam indicated (the vet's words, not mine) she wasn't pregnant, just over rehabilitated.

When faced with a choice of fodder, a goat will *never* pick scrub brush or weeds. Riley's favorite fare is horse grain, hay, and roses, roses, and roses.

Once upon a time, I had the most beautiful rose garden on my street. Now I have the best patch of scrub brush you ever saw. And I know for a fact that scrub is not on the goat's list of edible items!

# *You Named a Horse after a Vampire?*

LeStat was an interesting case study (doesn't that sound nice and clinical?). He came to us by way of the horse auction in Agawam, Massachusetts. It was spring, and he was lean and hungry from a hard winter. His coat was starved dull, and his feet had overgrown a set of racing shoes. The meat man barely looked up when he came out—not enough flesh to tempt (meat prices were down, and there was a glut of horses on the market). Bidding started out low and crested at $200. Now the meat man was interested; he could smell enough profit in the margin. He perked up his ears and made a bid of $210. The woman who had bid the $200 checked her wallet and sighed. All she had with her was $220. She really hadn't planned on buying today; she came up to check out the condition of the herd being offered.

"Well, here goes nothing" she thought, "$220."

The auctioneer looked back at the meat man, he glanced again at the horse, contemplated margins and shrugged, then shook his head *no*. There would be plenty more coming out at the same price with more meat on their bones. He could afford to wait. He'd get all he cared to buy tonight.

The money changed hands, a blank title was turned over, and the horse was loaded into a friend's trailer for the trip back to Connecticut. He boarded the trailer as if he'd done it many times before and rode quietly with no fuss during the hour trip back to The Last Refuge.

"This one will be easy to place," she thought. "If the rest of his manners and training are like what he's already displayed, and he vets out okay, he should be in a new home by summer."

Jane had been admiring the rescue efforts of The Last Refuge and had decided to "help out" by providing a new one to handle. She planned on covering all his expenses and get her feet wet with this first rescue trial.

"This isn't so hard," she said to me. "He'll be easy—you'll see."

I looked over the small, dark bay horse and noticed two things immediately: He had a tattoo inside his upper lip and the most devilish gleam in his eyes that it has ever been my misfortune to see.

"I think he's a registered standard breed, but those eyes don't promise easy," I responded.

"Oh, you never think easy," Jane answered back. "Don't worry so much. I'll find him a new home in no time at all."

We put him in the quarantine paddock for the night and planned on calling the vet in the morning to come out and vet check, start shots, and do worm counts.

Sometime over the next few hours, he got bored with the hay and water he'd been provided with and looked for something to occupy his time. Noticing the mares two fields over, he took down his fence and strolled over to make their acquaintance. They were not enamored with his looks or manners, and the gelding keeping them company took exception to the new horse's bulging challenge. The melee that ensued woke up the whole place, and our poor vet had to make a 3:30 a.m. barn call to clean, suture, and start tetanus shots. He had gotten banged up pretty thoroughly, but he had gotten his licks in, as well. Unfortunately his chosen method of retaliation included teeth, as well as front feet, but the gelding had chunks taken out of him.

"Well, Carol," my vet said with unholy relish, "this time you've gone and brought a vampire in. Watch out for full moons!" I looked over at Jane and winced. The gleam in her eye told me a pun was brewing.

"The Vampire LeStat—that's his name, all right," she crowed. "At least his spirit isn't crushed."

The vet and I shuddered. More than the peace of one night was going to be shattered by this one's arrival.

He soon proved us right. If there was a nail exposed, a fence board not on completely, a hole in the ground, anything and everything a horse could find to get hurt on, LeStat found it. To this day, I'm convinced my vet picked a bright yellow first aid cream for this horse based on his own obscure sense of humor. Black Icthamol or even a clear cream would have blended so much better with LeStat's almost black hide than the brilliant canary yellow ointment did. For awhile there, he looked like a surrealistic impression of a horse "painted" with sunshine. It certainly made it easy for frequent visitors to glance at him and know whether or not to ask what he had found to get hurt on this time.

He finally bounced back from his injuries with a vengeance (or perhaps he just ran out of places that needed repair). Anyway, he did more for helping us update routine maintenance than any other two horses ever have. But he still had so many stallion traits that we had his hormone levels checked to make sure he really was a gelding and not cut proud—that is, a stallion with retained gonads.

The test came back normal. He was physically gelded, but no one had ever informed his brain of the fact. He was small but he was mighty.

The first time he moved out across the field, pacing perfectly without breaking stride, we just knew he had to have been raced. We called and got his registry information, based on the lip tattoo, and sure enough, he had raced for several years before his last registered owner sold him on open market (she retained his papers and it cost Jane more to expedite the transfer of papers then she paid for the horse), and as near as we could track, he had been in several homes over the next few years, each one of them a little more on the wrong side of the track than the last. Ending up at the horse auction in Agawam was pretty near the end of the road for him, and he was only eight at the time.

He and Jane make a good pair (the good home she found him turned out to be her own), but we still can't trust him not to challenge any other gelding that stands between him and a field of mares. He also still retains his title as the best tester of a horse-safe area I've ever seen. If there's anything anywhere that can hurt a horse, or be broken by a horse, he will be the one to get in the middle of it. Plus, sometimes on a full moon, I'm convinced I hear wings flapping as the vampire comes out.

# *Tasmanian Hooligan*

It's one of those Darwinian wonders that, for most species, size seems to be in inverse proportion to spirit. Humans even have a phrase for it SMS (small man syndrome). If Saint Bernards had the drive and tenacity of some of the small terrier breeds, we'd all be cowering in terror. Pound for pound, a lion has nothing over the average house cat, so it should be no surprise to note that the coming of a very small pony to my farm would mark the beginning of the end of tranquility for the larger horses, and the start of an unusual "baby-sitting" chore for Chipper.

I've never seen a pony as small as the one that arrived in the back of that delivery van, or one as dirty. The driver said, "I've got a real project for you." He opened the back doors and let out a tiny, tattered terror. Even with over-grown feet, half starved and covered with moth-eaten hair, the light in Taz's eyes said there was *spirit* here. He bounced when he moved, and immediately he charged the fence, screaming defiance at the watching herd. They all looked down their noses at him and laughed. Taz stomped his feet and dared them to make fun of him. They laughed harder, and a gleam lit up the back of his eyes that promised revenge. The van driver laughed and said he'd be back to see all the action. He promised me excitement and took off, leaving me staring at this pint-sized morsel that was throwing a major temper tantrum.

My chocolate Lab, Chip, went to make friends, and Taz took one look at a dog almost his own size and decided that here was fun! Of course, a pony's idea of fun is not necessarily a dog's, and poor Chip was faced with a holy terror chasing him around, spinning and whirling like a dervish. Such was the entry of Taz, the Tasmanian Devil, into our life.

Taz was so small that none of my normal "horse deterrent" barriers deterred him. You should have seen the look on Lady's face when he scooted under her belly and stuck his nose in her feed bin. He would stir the whole herd up, get them chasing him over a hill, drop and roll under a fence, then stand on the other side, stomping and shouting at them. Poor Chip spent half his days rounding up the Taz and coaxing him back under the fence. After awhile, Chip employed Taz's favorite game of tag to accomplish this. Chip would "tag" Taz, then run as fast as he could for the fence, drop and roll under, and head for the pond. Taz would drop and follow, screeching to a halt at the pond's edge. Taz hated water. Chip would sit in the water and wait for rescue. Sooner or later, one of the horses would go shoo Taz out of the way, and a sodden Chipper would come back to tell me all about how bad Taz had been and how—poke, poke—*he* deserved dog biscuits for taking care of the monster. I felt so sorry for Chip until I watched him initiate the action, jump in the pond, and take off for the house, shouting for his reward.

By the end of Taz's recuperation, he and Chip would play by the hour with an old piece of rope. Each would grab an end and tug. Of course, Taz far outweighed Chip and could drag him around the yard by the rope anytime he wanted. Most of the time, though, he'd let Chip win, and Chip was convinced he was the best and baddest tug-of-war champ in the world. That conviction has led to some unforeseen events involving apron strings, but what is life without some fun? (The day he took me and the Thanksgiving turkey for a "pull" made for some excitement—on the part of our guests.)

The people who took Taz as a companion for their elderly horses (also alumni from here) were concerned that he might be bored there but fortunately he immediately taught their golden retrievers all his favorite games, and they tell me that he has graduated to sharing dog biscuits with them on the back deck. It sounds as if Taz was once a dog—probably a terrier! Chip was sorry to see him go but he perked up when I brought home some baby chickens for him to raise. Unfortunately they came as eggs, and he was the first thing they saw when they hatched and they imprinted on him! But that's a story for another day. It's late, and Chip has beat me to the bed. Let's see if I can convince him to share. Where are those biscuits?

# *The Fine Art of Stain Removal and Other Horse Ownership Facts*

Sometimes there is a calm that falls over the land in the gentle dusk of a quiet day as the hour hand climbs the left side of the clock. A time for reflection, perhaps even a little socialization in front of the television. Saturday night, this past weekend, offered a rare opportunity to do just that. I was just settled in, surrounded by dogs and family, television clicker rules established, and the sponsor spots came on. The guys tuned them out, but I was caught up short by the first one that came on. It showed people in clean, spotless clothes—eating, drinking, and playing Frisbee with a dog on a gently sloping grass lawn. Faintly seen behind the house were the well-kept fields and barn of a working farm. The lady of the house was voicing over how use of X laundry soap kept all her men's work clothes spotless, intact, and I'm pretty sure something about environmentally friendly bubbles was also mentioned. Then her clothes danced on the line and were kissed by the sun! Wow, I have to get me some of this stuff.

I was not unhappy that the guys didn't notice the ad's promises. As I looked at their clothes, I was struck by how much of our history is written in the shades of our stains. Let me just grab a few garments from the laundry basket and explore the colors of my days. We'll do Stain Analysis 101, and the textbook will be: my husband's shirt, ball cap and jeans, plus my shirt, pants, and jacket from Saturday. It was a calm, light day…how many new shades could the clothes have?

The ball cap: As I examine the cap, I realize that not only is the rim scruffy, muddy brown and green, but there also appears to be dried teeth marks embedded in it. It looks as if Mickey was playing "Keep Away" with my husband again. The rules are fairly straightforward: Steal hat, run away with it, drop it on the ground, pick it up, give it back, steal hat…but the execution can be unique each time. Do we drop the hat in the mud? Or in a pond? Do we clear the grass, bringing debris out of our mouth before we steal the hat? Or use it as a napkin? Sometimes the after-play cap reminds me of a tie-dyed garment; sometimes it doesn't even resemble a cap. This one falls in the middle range, a soggy and stained but still recognizable ball cap that has toured at least one ditch and a grass meadow today.

A man's plaid shirt, size large: Thank goodness for plaid. It disguises inadvertent deposits of "natural vegetable dyes" so well. Looking at this one, I can see my husband's day took him up close and personal to machine oil (tractor), gear grease (bush hog), cream gravy (lunch), grass (mowing the back field), and some kind of unidentified brown substance (hope it's mud). His jeans also confirm that he spread manure (don't ask), strung fencing, and cleaned out the drainage ditch. Now these clothes may not dance like the ones in the ad, but they can sure stand up in the corner by themselves.

A woman's denim shirt, size medium: Denim is one of those interesting fabrics that acquires "character" as it ages. It softens in texture and color with repeated washings. That provides a perfect canvas for "horse art." This small tear is from Rico, grabbing the back of the shirt and yanking me backwards into the water trough. That irregular area of beige is from a previous attempt to scrub grunge out of the sleeve. This orange spot is actually carrot slobber. That pink one is apple. And the half-torn off, downward-facing pocket is the result of a small miscalculation of how much of me could fit through the gap between two strands of the fence. My beige chino pants were not supposed to be part of this discussion; they are "work away from home" clothes and should not have been worn out into the field. But I was only going out for just a few minutes and how dirty could they get? Right, and I just love figuring out how to get these kinds of stains out of work clothes. I wish they would make business attire out of Teflon. It would certainly save me when I decide to go out and play with the babies before I change. Sometimes I feel as if I'm back in grade school ("Change into your play clothes as soon as you get home!") except, at least then, I had the excuse of personal growth rather than stain growth for the purchase of new clothes. Needless to say, this particular pair of chinos have been "released from the work force" and will now share the ever-expanding realm of multi-hued farm-only clothes.

A woman's jacket, size baggy-saggy: I think this jacket was once beige heather-green. I can't remember since it has been awhile since any portion of the original color remained intact to entice me with how beautiful it was. I do recollect that this jacket was going to be a wear-to-work jacket, a classic, timeless addition to my business attire that would coordinate with other useful, neutral-shaded accessories. I don't even have a horse on the property that is neutral shaded. What made me think my clothes would stay that way?

I'm going to have to go look at that ad again. It's as close as I'll ever get to clean, spotless clothes that are more than a few days old. But then again, I don't remember seeing any horses in those immaculate fields of green, rolling into hills behind the barn, either.

# *Silhouettes in the Noonday Haze*

One Wednesday in May 2003, over 40 horses, donkeys, cows, and a llama were seized in a neglect case in Galveston County, Texas. I have elected not to include the name of their owner in this story—suffice it to say, she had owned several of them from 1993 on, and complaints against their condition had prompted multiple calls on her by the local humane society and animal control officer. Both agencies had offered to help her and the animals, volunteering support, assistance, food, shelter, and so forth, for the animals' use. She refused, however. She was adamant that there was no problem with her herd. The weather turned warm very early, and temperatures in the high 90s were recorded. The herd waited under what little shelter the heat-scorched trees afforded, as they watched their sick and elderly members die, one by one. No one came to help until a thirteen-year-old girl, on her way to church, passed down the little-used lane in front of the farm and noticed there were dead horses in the field. With tearful eyes and pleading voice, she called Habitat for Horses and reported what she had seen. After too long an investigation period, a court order to seize them was signed.

When the animals were seized, the workers took great care to search the woods, fields, and piles of decaying garbage lying around. No one wanted to leave any animal behind. Skeletons peeked out of makeshift graves, and bits of fur dangled from dead tree branches. Just as the last of the trucks was preparing to leave, a small donkey dragged himself out of the woods. He was so sad; even his eyes bled pain. Several of the volunteers stood by him for a long time when they got to the ranch, petting and hugging him. The vet said the wounds were caused by wild dogs that he valiantly fought alone and, in pain, offering his life in defense of his herd.

Shortly after the seizure, I went over to the Habitat for Horses and saw the volunteers laboring in the hot, humid haze of over 90-degree weather. Around them in small paddocks milled a frightened assortment of donkeys, miniature horses and donkeys, full-sized horses, and cows. These were the debris of man's inhumanity, washed up on the shores of indifference. Walking hunks of hair, bleeding sores, wrapped around sore, swollen skeletons. They looked like animated, two-dimensional beings. The only juxtaposition into substance was the heartbreak of angular hips and vertebrae-counting spines. They were the discards of our throwaway society. One of the most robust, a fifteen-hand quarter horse, was taped at less than 610 pounds. (Normally, a fifteen-hand quarter horse in good conditions weighs over 1100 pounds; taping uses a special tape measure that wraps around a horse at the withers and, employing a formula, calculates the weight of the horse.)

Swollen-bellied mares with matchstick limbs tottered around in one area, stepping carefully around spindly babies that were dropping down in the shade for noonday naps. Minis, harlequin donkeys, Arabs, quarter horses, pregnant and just-foaled mothers had heads buried in bins of fresh hay; others were soaking down gallons of needed water. Eyes stared dully out from sunken, cavernous sockets.

Ungelded males stared across as their mares and babies revived. A donkey jack tottered on jester-tilted, high-heeled feet toward the water trough in his paddock, which was being lovingly refilled by a young girl. A group of young men cleaned an area under the watchful eye of a flattened cow with a calf tugging wistfully at her empty udder. From under the volunteer tent, a motherly woman was offering a bottle for the baby.

Recalling the horrors of that afternoon, I see the silhouette of a man in the distant haze; his head is bowed, his shoulders silently shaking. He is bent over the small body of a donkey at final rest, curled on the ground with nose to tail, as if it were a small dog in sleep. I hear him say through a tear-wrecked voice, "I'm so sorry, little one. Rest now." The donkey's tongue has slipped forward exposing a tremendous gash that was inexpertly stitched and left to fester too many painful weeks ago. This is the donkey that dragged himself out of the woods a few days ago, hearing the voice of rescue and determined to come for help. He watched as his brethren were picked up and made safe. He saw the tears, heard the soft words of comfort, and he met the man and his vet who wanted so much for him to live. He felt the gentle hand of the man who promised him anything if he would try for just another day, another hour. He was so tired, though, from all the days of vigil, of keeping his herd together. He saw they were safe, and he lay down. He looked toward safety and went on, leaving only the man to stand over his discarded body and weep.

The haze obscures their silhouettes, or maybe it's my tears.

# *Credo*

It is evening, and work has ended for the day. The sounds of agony are stilled for the moment. A false calm has come to the busy slaughterhouse. Huddled in feed lots outdoors, the momentary survivors of today's bloodshed nuzzle each other for comfort as their eyes glaze with unshed tears for those lost to them. I see them behind my eyes; they march through my dreams, their hooves providing the beat as the Proclaimers sing "500 Miles."

I have read of everyone's disgust and anger at what is occurring, I have heard the fists cleaving air as they thrust upward to the heavens. Such an inordinately large number of us are dedicated to stopping slaughter. I can hear the Proclaimers' refrain ringing in my head:

"But I would walk 500 miles
And I would walk 500 more
Just to be the man who walked 1,000 miles
To fall down at your door."

Every morning, I startle awake from my tear-drenched pillow and remember the lost, and I mourn the ones that will face today's debacle. I hear the soft, waking sounds of lightly dreaming horses and pray they will escape the river too soon engulfing them. When I wake up, I want to be next to horses and see them safe and with their friends. Instead. I wake to the horror creeping behind my head. More will drip their lifeblood in slow, agonizing drops today.

"When I wake up yeah I know I'm gonna be
I'm gonna be the man who wakes up next to you
When I go out yeah I know I'm gonna be
I'm gonna be the man who goes along with you."

I bathe my reddened eyes, swallow coffee as bitter as my regrets, and head off to work. I dedicate my day and the salary it produces to stopping this outrage.

"When I'm working yes I know I'm gonna be
I'm gonna be the man who's working hard for you
And when the money comes in for the work I'll do
I'll pass almost every penny on to you."

When I get home, there are noses to kiss and promises to make. I would walk 500 miles, and I would walk 500 more. Just to be the man who walked 1,000 miles to fall down at your door. All this I would do to keep the horses safe.

"When I come home oh I know I'm gonna be
I'm gonna be the man who comes back home to you
And if I grow old well I know I'm gonna be
I'm gonna be the man who's growing old with you."

I was deeply disturbed by the poll about slaughter that was just done by a major horse magazine—not about the percentages but about how few people responded. Less than three thousand people took the time to respond to the question. That is a fractional percentage too small to be statistically significant. Do so few people care? Is everyone too busy, too shy, too full of "good intentions, but with no follow-through"? Where is the passion, the outrage, where is the presence of our desire? One-on-one, people say to me they care, yet the union of that feeling has yet to occur. In unity only is there strength.

"But I would walk 500 miles
And I would walk 500 more
Just to be the man who walked 1,000 miles
To fall down at your door."

We cannot all walk 500 miles literally but figuratively we should all be on our way down the road to stop slaughter, roaring our disapproval, shaking the doors of Congress, demanding this law be passed now—not next year, not next month, but now! Otherwise, it could come to pass that communion with horses may become outdated, encased in the Smithsonian next to the passenger pigeon. The horse census is dropping in the world. Slaughter reduces numbers daily. I do not want my grandchildren to only dream of horses. I do not want the wonderful scent of horses to fade from our memories, the poetry of their movement captured only on ancient film.

"When I'm lonely yes I know I'm gonna be
I'm gonna be the man who's lonely without you
When I'm dreaming well I know I'm gonna dream
Dream about the time when I'm with you."

The time grows near when everyone must choose—get off that fence and stand to be counted. Martin Luther King, Jr., softly proclaimed, "I have a dream"—and the world changed. I am preparing to face the enemy in our legislature and demand to be heard. I too have a dream. My dream is to stop the nightmare. Who stands with me? Who will affirm that

"I too would walk 500 miles
And I would walk 500 more
Just to be the man who walked 1,000 miles
To fall down at your door."

With our affirmation, we will shake the doors of Congress and the very halls of justice will resound to the cadence of our tread. We will be heard and before the day is over, slaughter will be outlawed. In unity is strength. Here is my hand in pledge, who will offer theirs?

# *Each Horse's Death Diminishes Me*

The following is a eulogy that was read at a candlelit vigil in Houston, Texas, honoring the many horses that were slaughtered for human consumption in that state. Picture a crowd gathered in front of a fountain with the sunset bouncing from one tall glass spire to another, igniting the faces of the people with rosy hues. They are holding candles, and a ship's bell sounds the refrains for the horses lost. Many mounted police surround the crowd, keeping it encircled. As the eulogy is read, some of it echoing the words of poets John Donne and T. S. Eliot, some wipe their eyes and others look down. I choke up as I read the list of nameless, lost horses.

*Start with a ringing of bells, then*

I dream of horses.

Each evening as the sun softly sets, turning the clouds to trailing glories of orange, gold, lavender, and crimson, I gently kiss my herd goodnight. I turn and go in, with a last glance at the contented herd as it moves off toward the cool water in the pond and then goes to graze on the sweet grass. Each one is different, as unique as all my fellow Texans are.

Some of us were lucky enough to be born here; others got here as soon as we could.

Some of us came here for opportunities and horse dreams; others came in agony and despair.

Some of us live the life of the free; others daily face the reality of being torn from all we know and love, of watching them march through a door that exudes pain, moans, finality…watch and wait for our turn.

I see questions: "Who is this *we*?"

"We are not animals, not horses. We are humans. Slaughter affects only the animals, and we own them. It is our right!"

"Who is this woman to speak of *we*?"

"It's only other people's horses they are coming for; her horses are safe."

"If she is that concerned, let her take care of her own, and leave the rest of us alone."

"*We?* There is no *we* in this topic."

During a time of shame, Martin Niemoller wrote:

"They came for the communists, and I did not speak up because I wasn't a communist.

They came for the socialists, and I did not speak up because I was not a socialist.

They came for the union leaders, and I did not speak up because I wasn't a union leader.

They came for the Jews, and I didn't speak up because I wasn't a Jew.

Then they came for me, and there was no one left to speak up for me."

I say *we* because if I don't, my horse dreams will be nightmares…bells will toll instead of ring. The sunset will not be followed by a sunrise, and the grass will grow rank and coarse, and there will be no more goodnight kisses from my babies. And I will *not* go gently into this good night. I will rage, rage against the dying of the light.

It is another beautiful evening, and I have left my herd to come here and share the dusk with you. As we light our candles, let us remember why we are here. Let us memorialize those that have passed on to the gentle slopes and sweet dreams on the other side of the Rainbow. Let their passing be mourned but let it also serve as a pledge. After tonight, let all our thoughts be united to say, "They came for our horses and we said, *No!*"

Now, please light your candles and help me remember those that are here in spirit only, the more than 150 that die each day. I dream horse dreams, and each horse that dies takes a little of the splendor out of my world. Each horse's death diminishes me.

## The Tolling Of The Bells

Each horse's death diminishes me,
For I am involved in horse kind.
Therefore, send not to know
For whom the bell tolls,
It tolls for thee.

> Oh, the bells, bells, bells!
> What a tale their terror tells
> Of Despair!
>
> How they clang, and clash, and roar!
> What a horror they outpour.

A reading of the last legacy of some who have perished...their remains consumed, their eyes dimmed, their sole epitaph until now only a description written on a piece of paper, with a dollar sign next to it

A gelding, 5, quarter horse, shod **(bell tolls once)**

A gelding, 7, quarter horse, no brand **(bell tolls once)**

A mare, 9, thoroughbred bay with a white blaze and lip tattoo **(bell tolls once)**

A gelding, frozen to death in a double-decker trailer on the way to Canada; he was called the Popsicle horse in the papers. **(bell tolls once)**

A mare, 11, pregnant, no brand **(bell tolls once)**

A load of 9, 1 bad, unable to stand **(bell tolls once)**

A yearling, roan, under 500 pounds **(bell tolls once after each horse that follows)**

A bay thoroughbred gelding, 15hh

A sorrel mustang gelding, 14hh, auction tag #37

A bay quarter horse filly, 13hh

A sorrel, roan and white paint filly, 13hh

A bay quarter horse pony mare, 13hh

A sorrel quarter horse filly, 13hh

A bay mustang gelding, 14hh, auction tag #1043

A bay thoroughbred stallion, 16hh

A bay mustang gelding, 14hh, auction tag #45

A bay thoroughbred gelding, 15hh

A bay pony gelding, 13hh

A brown quarter horse mare, 14hh

A bay thoroughbred gelding, 16hh

A chestnut thoroughbred filly, 14hh

A bay quarter horse mare, 16hh

A bay mustang gelding, 14hh, auction tag #51

A bay mustang gelding, 15hh, auction tag #1053

A brown mustang gelding, 14hh, auction tag #54

A sorrel quarter horse colt, 13hh

A bay thoroughbred mare, 16hh

A bay mustang gelding, 13hh, auction tag #57

A grey quarter horse mare, 14hh

A bay quarter horse gelding, 14hh

A brown quarter horse filly, 13hh

A bay quarter horse gelding, 14hh

A dun quarter horse mare, 14hh

A sorrel quarter horse stallion, 14hh

A gray quarter horse gelding, 16hh

A bay quarter horse gelding, 14hh

A chestnut thoroughbred mare, 15hh

A sorrel quarter horse gelding, 14hh

A dun paint mare, 15hh

A sorrel paint gelding, 15hh

A bay quarter horse gelding, 15hh

A sorrel and white paint mare, 15hh

A sorrel quarter horse mare, 15hh

A sorrel draft gelding, 17hh

A gray thoroughbred mare, 16hh

A sorrel quarter horse colt, 13hh

A sorrel quarter horse gelding, 14hh

A bay quarter horse mare, 15hh

A sorrel quarter horse gelding, 14hh

A gray Appaloosa gelding, 14hh

A sorrel quarter horse gelding, 15hh

A sorrel quarter horse gelding, 14hh

A bay quarter horse mare, 15hh; brand category: "LD"

A sorrel quarter horse mare, 14hh

A bay Appaloosa mare, 15hh

A bay quarter horse mare, 15hh

A sorrel quarter horse mare, 16hh

A sorrel and white paint mare, 14hh

A sorrel quarter horse gelding, 15hh

A sorrel quarter horse gelding, 14hh

A dun quarter horse colt, 14hh

A black quarter horse colt, 13hh

A bay quarter horse colt, 13hh, branded

A paint colt, 14hh

A sorrel quarter horse colt, 12hh

A bay and white Appaloosa colt, 13hh

A gray quarter horse filly, 13hh; branded

A black quarter horse colt, 13hh

A sorrel quarter horse colt, 12hh

A bay quarter horse filly, 13hh

A bay quarter horse mare, 15hh; branded

A sorrel quarter horse gelding, 14hh; branded

A palomino gelding, 15hh; branded

A brown quarter horse gelding, 15hh; branded

A bay quarter horse gelding, 15hh; branded

A gray quarter horse gelding, 15hh; branded

A bay quarter horse gelding, 15hh; branded

A bay quarter horse mare, 16hh; branded

A bay quarter horse gelding, 15hh; branded

A dun quarter horse mare, 15hh; branded

A black mustang gelding, 14hh, auction tag #94

## Bells ring slowly three times

"What is that sound high in the air
Murmur of maternal lamentation
Who are those hooded hordes swarming
Over endless plains, stumbling in cracked earth
Ringed by the flat horizon only?"

## Bells ring slowly three times:

Oh, the bells, bells, bells!
What a tale their terror tells
Of Despair!

How they clang, and clash, and roar!
What a horror they outpour
(What a horror they outpour)

## Trumpet is heard playing taps in background

Day is done, gone the sun,
From the hills, from the lakes,
From the sky.
Horses all, safely rest,
Rescue is near by.

Go to sleep, peaceful sleep,
Be thee stallion or pretty mare,
Let us keep.
On the land without a care,
Safe in sleep.

Love, good night. Must thou go,
When the day, and the night
Need thee so?
All is well. Speedeth all
To their rest.

Fades the light, and afar
Goeth day, and the stars
Shineth bright,
Fare thee well; day has gone,
Night is on.

Thanks and praise, for our days,
'Neath the sun, 'neath the stars,
'Neath the sky,
As we go, this we know,
Rescue is near by.

# *The Bison*

The coming of TJ to my place aroused major curiosity from my neighbors. He came in the spring, half-bald and shedding massive amounts of dense, curly hair. Even his mane and tail were moth-eaten. At the time I acquired TJ, my vet was betting he'd never see thirty again, and if his teeth were any indication (all four of them), he was probably on the sunny side of thirty-five.

TJ was old, decrepit, and had been rescued from the meat truck by a woman who loved him dearly. Unfortunately, she could no longer afford him, and the stable where he had been was using him as a lesson horse to cover his board. Poor ole TJ was arthritic and sore, yet he gamely carried neophyte riders around the ring until he was too sore to limp anymore. His owner was informed he could no longer work for board, and she had to find somewhere else for him. After a hasty call from her, TJ came here and here he stays.

As spring dissolved into summer heat, TJ shed no more. He lugged his woolly body around the field, disappearing into the pond during the noonday heat. I couldn't stand it any more by the end of June, so TJ got shorn. His coat was so immense the horse clippers couldn't get through it, and I was reduced to using sheep shears on him, but he emerged sleek looking and cool. "Well, he probably hadn't been shed out in eons," I thought. "Next spring won't be nearly as bad."

TJ moped around all summer, and it was touch and go whether he would make it into his first winter with me. I stocked plenty of senior horse help to get TJ through the winter as fall set in. Winter in Connecticut is hard on senior horses and the fear of colic is ever-present. TJ looked at the weather and proceeded to grow a coat that was twice as shaggy as the one he came with, more curly, and denser than sheep wool. He loved being in the snow, and he scorned the bitter winds. In fact, he got downright frisky as the winter rolled over us. The colder it got, the shaggier TJ grew. The rumor at the grocery store was that The Last Refuge had a bison running with the horses. Several cars pulled up to see the buffalo, and the local school called to ask me whether it was true. Could they bring the kids on a field trip? I finally posted a sign on the bulletin board at the grocery store to explain that under all that hair was a horse—not a bison.

After the spring thaw, TJ proceeded to imitate a moth-eaten coat again. Out came the sheep shears, and the sleek TJ emerged again to start growing his coat all over again. This cycle has continued for four years, and the "shearing of the sheep" in the spring includes my "bison."

The curls and wool of TJ, his spring baldness, gentle temperament, and longevity are attributable to his being a Bashkir Curly. There are approximately 2000 of these horses in America. How one of them ended up as a job horse is one of those mysterious twists of fate that sometimes just occurs.

# A Home for Star

Star arrived into this world in spite of the best efforts of men to prevent it. His mother, The Golden One (TGO, for short), had been a hack horse (rented out to people by the hour to use as they saw fit) for over ten years. She is a small quarter horse-Arabian cross with the true palomino coloring of new-minted gold with a flaxen mane and tail. My understanding is that when she arrived at the stable, she was a sweet tempered, anxious-to-please horse. After the first few years of dragging loads over hills, however, she turned into the most ill-tempered, obstinate beast I'd ever met. She was mean and stubborn, and she would lie down and roll on an unwary rider. The workers at the stable quickly learned she had the fastest hind feet in the world and didn't hesitate to use them on anyone who crossed her. The Golden One could—and would—spin and kick before you could blink.

My first introduction to this blond bombshell was infelicitous but definitely exhilarating. Lady and I were sauntering through the local park enjoying the fine spring weather—and each other—when over the hill careened an out-of-control horse with a terrified rider barely on her back. TGO took one look at the two of us and decided we were a threat. As sinuously as a snake, she slithered out from under her rider, wheeled and spun, planting one back hoof on Lady's rump and the other one squarely on my thigh. With a snake-headed glare of defiance and a snort, she tore off, leaving utter chaos in her wake. Lady didn't unseat me during the rumpus, but in the process of her terrified rearing and plunging, my nose got hit and started to bleed. To make matters worse, the hapless "lessee" of TGO had sprained an ankle in the ruckus. She couldn't walk back to the barn, and she wouldn't ride TGO back. There was no way I was getting on that particular horse's back, so Lady condescended to cart the injured rider, and I got to limp over to the hack stable leading Lady and TGO (leering and sneering at each other the whole way back). I was so impatient to give that "sweet" mare back to her rightful owners that I jogged part of the way. I handed her over to an unwilling barn helper and got out of there.

That should have been the end of this story except someone up there loves a joke. About five months later, my phone rang, and the ACO (Animal Control Officer) was on the line and told me about a horse that needed help: A mare (very pregnant) was at a riding stable, had had with no prenatal care, and she was extremely sick and needed to be placed. There was nothing to be said except, "Bring her over. I'll call the vet." An hour later, his truck arrived towing a rocking and swaying trailer. Off it staggered a rib-thin, belly-swollen, evil-eyed TGO. My jaw dropped, and poor Lady looked over the fence and tore off to the back pasture, screaming warnings to the others. The ACO snickered, handed me the lead rope, and said, "This one is all yours. The stable already signed her over. Good luck." He was smart to leave immediately because if my hands weren't full of angry horse, they would have been full of his hair!

When our horse-savvy vet arrived, he took one look at TGO and refused to touch her without sedation. To make matters worse, he announced she was imminently due to deliver, and if he wasn't mistaken, he'd been told that the coming foal's father was the Arabian stallion that had broken one of the other local vet's legs. "That's why the stable dumped her on you, Carol. Find this one a new home as fast as you can." With those cheery words, he departed. I got her settled in the foaling stall and got out before the tranquilizer wore off. That night, she snake-headed everyone who walked into the barn, as well as any horse that dared look her way.

I went back up to house muttering to myself things that I won't write here. My husband went out to check on her and came back saying how beautiful and sweet she was. I asked him if he had looked at the right horse, and he said, "The blond—right? She's wonderful!"

There was a feverish gleam in his eyes and a softness to his expression as he spoke of TGO. I inquired of him where in the head had he been kicked, and he looked at me as if I was crazy. Then the unmentionable came out of his mouth, the dreaded words "I always wanted a palomino horse, and she looks like just the ticket." Still muttering to myself, I went to bed leaving him up dreaming of a name for his perfect girl.

The next morning TGO greeted us with Star at her side. It didn't take her long to get the lay of the land and decide it was okay to foal here. My husband cooed, chortled, and stroked TGO. She leaned into him and leered at me over his shoulder.

"Isn't she just the perfect girl?" he chuckled. "This one is staying with Daddy, aren't you, TGO?"

I offered to dye my hair blond if that's what it took, but he insisted, and TGO is with us to this day. For your information, she has never kicked my husband and broken only ribs on me once, so I guess you could say it's a success. I still won't walk in a stall with her, but we have reached an understanding since Lady grew up and trounced her once. TGO doesn't lay a hoof or tooth on any of my new "rescues," and only occasionally does she vent her anger on the old-timers. The fact that she is never ridden and just gets to lie around looking beautiful has brought back a lot of sweetness to her nature, but the snake lies close to the surface, waiting to strike again.

Star is a buckskin and inherited his mother's intelligence, his father's fiery temperament, and his mother's back feet. If one could say a child got the worst of both parents, Star would be that one. Before he was six weeks old, he popped over a fence and challenged an old gelding for supremacy. Too smart for his own good, and too cocky to care, he dared the world to make him mind. And his mother stood right behind him, backing him up on all his whims.

This is not a place for the young horses. If they're fit and ready to take their place in the world of horses, there are homes waiting for them, and they all go forth to them. It was always understood that once weaned, Star would have a new home. People normally wean horses at four to six months or, if left alone, the mother will wean them at somewhere around nine months. Not TGO—she would have nursed him till he was old and toothless. She had fought hard to have this baby and she wasn't giving him up easily. The only reason that Star was finally weaned was that, hard-hearted me, I separated them when Star was twenty-one months old.

By two and a half, Star had grown into a small, compact, tremendously athletic horse. It was time to find him a new home. This was easier said than done. Everyone who came to see him raved about his looks, but hated his personality. He is extremely intelligent, and he figured out rapidly that I wouldn't give him to anyone who wasn't "right" for him. My friend Greg came over to help me teach him to trailer, and Star (the brat that he is) proceeded to leap out of the trailer over the divider and through the back gap, neatly tucking his legs and slithering out. Greg looked at me and said I should advertise him as green, willing, and does four feet in trailers. When I looked puzzled, he explained that maybe someone would think it was a misprint and meant four feet *and* trailers.

It appeared that Star would stay here forever, but one day a tiny woman came to visit. Barely four feet ten and extremely soft-spoken, Mary was looking for an elderly horse as a companion to her young mare. I liked her immediately, my vet vouched for her, and most important, my dog Chip approved of her. We went out to the barn discussing which ones were available for adoption when she stopped dead in her tracks. I looked at the mesmerized expression on her face and recognized the gape-jawed wonder in her eyes. It bore an uncanny similarity to the look in my husband's eyes when he watches TGO. Glancing over to see which one she was admiring, I was struck dumb by the sight of Star gazing back at her with the same look. I smiled and said, "Do I have the horse for you."

Mary and Star are now inseparable and treat each other with the same admiration as my husband and The Golden One. I guess it's true that for every horse there's just one perfect owner, and thank goodness these two found theirs. Now, if Lady would only forgive me for TGO still being here, The Last Refuge would be perfect too!

# *Barn Dreams*

Horse people have interesting quirks that identify us as a breed the minute we open our mouths in front of a knowledgeable listener. One of the easiest things to spot is the avid gleam in our eyes as we behold a lush, green lawn in the process of being mowed. The suspicion is confirmed when the first words we come out with are, "Oh boy, what a waste of beautiful grass. I have an environmentally friendly lawn mower I can bring over, no charge." I have non-horse friends (yes, it is possible for the two cultures to bridge the gap between them) who have been embarrassed to tears by my open-mouthed gaping at things that left them cold and unmoved. They just can't believe manure shovels, selling at 50 percent off, are something we have to run across three towns to pick up, and I don't think any of them are willing to go grocery shopping with me again. There's something about standing next to a shopping cart full of big bags of carrots and having to listen to "eyesight" jokes that leaves them unmoved.

Despite all that, our friendship has survived. They've actually gotten into cooking up huge pots of bran mash, sewing up horse blankets, and even helping pick apples for my current crowd every fall. The infamous night they came for a long-promised dinner—only to find the stove cold, nothing in the oven, and their hostess in the barn distraught over a sick horse—strained, but it didn't break our friendship. They cooked, served and cleaned up without even a hint of my reappearance onto the scene, and only occasionally do they bring up that fact (it's now down to once-a-day reminders). As I've said, our friendship has survived. Then the old barn roof blew away, and I started having "barn dreams," and we had a definite gap in communication.

Strained? Our friendship was bent, twisted, and frayed during the ensuing period. I walked around breathing, speaking, and acting on nothing but A New Barn. For women whose only interest in wood is the finish on their dining room tables to have to listen to non-stop talk of trusses, load-bearing capabilities, flooring, and so forth, is asking a lot. I dreamed *barn*, ate *barn*, lived *barn*. I was obsessed by new barn desires. Meanwhile, they yawned and promised each other that this too would pass.

My banker thought I was crazy when I came in for a home-improvement loan and displayed blue prints for a new barn—especially after his appraiser came back, saying what I really needed was a new well and the roof of the house replaced. He might have survived that, but when I responded, "The house roof will keep. Okay, a new well for the babies would be nice. But I'm really dreaming of a new barn, thank you," my poor banker just shook his head and suggested I come down to earth a little.

Come down to earth? Winter is coming—and I needed a new barn!

Fortunately, for the sanity of all, the matter resolved itself. We have a new barn, and now all I dream about is filling it with hay. My friends are standing up pretty well to discussions of first versus second cut, timothy versus alfalfa, but for some reason they are threatening to boycott any dinner parties arranged around hay delivery dates. I wouldn't ask them to throw up hay bales, but they could catch, couldn't they? It's great exercise and working together is so good for building friendship.

# *Mud Season*

Most people greet the first warm days of spring with great enthusiasm. Spring means flowers, warmth, and the end of snow. Each new glimpse of the promised awakening is cheered and paraded as a glad reason to think about an end to frozen, hard ground, and frozen-hard attitudes.

Those who live in the country also cheer the onslaught of spring. It's just that we have *another* season to get through first: Mud Season. Mud Season slides into view every year about the time we are fed up with winter and begging for any type of respite from the cold, relentless monotony of unfreezing buckets, mucking out stalls, comforting bored, cranky horses, treating frostbite, and too few hours later, starting all over again. For some reason, every year I forget that the first warm days of spring mean the ground thaws into a bog, a morass, and a mire for itchy, shedding horses to wallow in. I forget mercifully until it happens—and all of a sudden, the whole herd is brown. Then I remember what lies ahead, and I shudder.

Mud Season is the time of year when I go out into the field wearing two boots and return with one. The other gets sucked off my foot into the relentless, slurping mouth of the knee-deep mud. Mud Season steals horseshoes, as well, blithely lapping them off faster than my farrier can replace them. It swallows up any and all fancied offerings. I've stood amazed, watching as the very item I need most totally disappears from view with audible gulps of pleasure emitting from the mud.

Mud Season is insidious; it inserts its presence everywhere. My white and blue kitchen floor displays tan tones, brown smudges, and beige splashes. My barn wardrobe spends more time in the washer than anywhere else. Mud, muck, and mire creep into the house through every fancied crevice. Not even the chill winds of winter breach the walls of my house as thoroughly as does the slime of Mud Season.

Mud Season is the gawky, coltish period of the year. It is spring not grown into its legs yet, sprawling out over winter's beard, falling and giggling with glee. It is an adolescent with the mercurial temperament of a "horror-moan"-tossed teen. It's all sweetness one second, surging with fury the following, and it changes moods in spinning, dizzying promises of better behavior to follow.

And just when it all seems unbearable, the ground firms up, green breaks through, lost items are disgorged, and spring majestically strolls in the door. Mud Season—it's not so bad. It means spring is right around the corner.

# Clock Watching

At the barn where I used to board, the office was on the other side of the arena from the boarders' side. For the convenience of all, the owner installed a telephone bell to signal when a call was coming in. The first few times it sounded, a few of the horses looked up from their hay, but, after a brief moment of contemplation, the sound was accepted and ignored. We all adopted the same attitude to it, as well, and other than going to answer the summons, it was not something we considered.

One spring day, a new boarder came in with Dusty, a thoroughbred horse that she had just bought off the track. We gave her the first stall as it had Dutch doors and its own private paddock off the back. Dusty had never been with other horses and would need to be integrated into the herd slowly. This would give him the opportunity to "learn horse language" vicariously from the safety of his paddock. Like so many ex-racehorses, he was coming out of an environment of being in a stall twenty-three hours a day and out only for exercise. We all cautioned his new owner that the retraining process would be slow, and Dusty would need to settle in at his own pace.

Dusty came off the horse trailer wide-eyed and snorting. He did settle down some after he was placed in his new stall and, after blowing challenges at the horses in the field, he deigned to eat some hay. Just as we all were breathing a sigh, the owner called to see how Dusty was doing. Unfortunately, the forgotten telephone bell was mounted on the wall above Dusty's stall.

Dusty threw his head up, snorted "It's a race!" and turned and charged through the Dutch door into his paddock. As the remains of the door hit the ground, he hit the fence. Like all good athletes, it barely slowed him down. Littering the ground with fence debris, he hit the main field flying. The main herd pricked their ears, alerted, then saw the commotion, and took off. Dusty took one look at the herd disappearing over the hill in front of him, heard the "starting bell" pealing behind him and proceeded into the race of his life. As he hit the top of the hill, he was in the lead. The herd saw a new horse running and trumpeting challenges, and they took off after him. When I answered the phone and heard his new owner on the other end ask me how he was settling in, all I could answer was that he had been a little skittish but was in the process of "exploring" his new surroundings. And, oh yes, we were moving him to a quieter stall farther down the row. From that day forward, Dusty was known as the horse that raced the telephone.

# *Heave Ho*

I just had to share this with you all. Tonight I was a wee bit late getting out to the barn to feed. My Appaloosa cross, warm-blood horse, Lady (who, when she's not eight months pregnant, weighs 1400 pounds) decided to pop over the six-foot fence to come to see where I was. Because she was already out in forbidden territory, she made the most of her freedom—kicking heels, rolling, and just plain showing off all around the yard. All three dogs alerted me that there was something wrong in the back yard, and I went charging out with Bailer following me (he can open the slider, and I forgot to lock it in my haste).

Here it is dusk, and I'm calling Lady as I pull on my boots, hopping up and down on the deck (cold, snow, ice, and socks don't go well together). Bailer assumes the protector crouch in front of me, growling, baring teeth, and hackles raised. He's one ferocious dog. Now I'm hollering, "Down, Bailer! Here, Lady," and the rest of the herd is bellowing at me to come let them in and feed them *now*!

As the last boot goes on, through the dusk thundering toward me is one very large, very excited, and very pregnant horse. Bailer crouches lower, growls more ("I'll protect you, Mom"), Lady screams ("I'll get that dog that's menacing you, Mom") and thunders faster towards us. As her size becomes more apparent, Bailer's ears go up, and he turns and looks at me, licks my hand, and runs backwards through my legs. I fall down, sprawled at Lady's feet. She stops and reaches down, grabs the front of my sweater (fortunately, it is loose enough that she didn't get me too!) and hauls me upward. Bailer goes crazy ("She's eating Mom!"), leaps up, grabs hold of the back of my jeans, and starts hauling backwards. Now we have a tug of war over Mom!

All things being equal, weight finally won out and there we were: Bailer suspended from me, me from Lady—when around the house comes my husband with some dear friends who were coming to dinner. Lady drops me and runs over to see if they have any goodies in the bag they are carrying—as it hits the ground, along with their jaws. Bailer lets go and I follow. I quietly get up, dust myself off, and say, "So nice of you to drop by," then I lose it completely. Lady and Bailer each have an end of the same carrot and are busy trying to convince the other to drop it! My friends are having a field day with stories about dinner at Carol's. Guess I'd better get off and cook something, huh?

# *Pretty Is as Pretty Does*

When I was young (no, not quite a thousand years ago), I used to bemoan my looks to my grandmother. "I'll never be pretty like the other girls," I cried to her. Her response, "Pretty is as pretty does," did little to reassure me. I wanted golden curls, not straight, reddish-brown hair. I desired a small heart-shaped profile with rosebud lips and a soft little chin, but to a certainty the strong cheekbones and stubbornly jutted chin I had inherited didn't come close to that ideal.

As the years have passed, I've become reconciled to my looks but I have admittedly never outgrown my love of the physically beautiful, that symmetrical perfection granted to so few creatures in life. Maybe that's why horses captured my imagination at a very tender age. The flow of their forms as they float across a mist-enshrouded meadow, manes and tails flowing in defiance of gravity, as they appear to dance around the air molecules, slides effortlessly through the distance of my earliest memories and catches my breath up in the inarticulate awareness of their innate perfection.

That fierce desire for dream perfection that I grew out of is still very evident in the horse-owning community. Certainly not all, but more than a few people, have a preconceived notion of what a real horse is. The color may vary, but invariably the dream horse is young, vital, flowing in gaits, superbly equipped athletically, perfectly trained, and, of course, able to win any and all shows. However, just as very few humans match the perfect ideal, not all horses measure up. And even those that do inevitably grow older, and a little lame; bowed tendons develop, perfection fades, and reality is left. Regardless of how faithful the service rendered has been, many of these horses end up on the auction block, like a used car traded in for the newest, shiniest model available.

In Connecticut in the late 1990s, if one was willing to make the drive, there were multiple small auctions available to pick up cheap, well-used horses. At the time, there was a glut on the market, and the killer-buyers were not as hungry and avid as they had been in the past. Amfran, a French-Belgian slaughter plant, had shut down in Connecticut, and horses had to be trucked much farther, making inroads into their profits. This resulted in horses being able to be picked up fairly cheaply, and I often came back from auction with three or four, whereas before, I might be able to bring only one back. Instead of meat pricing being up to $400, the killer-buyers started shaking their heads after a bid of $200 went on a 1,000-pound horse.

At one auction, when Pretty Woman hit the auction floor, no one would bid above $25, and the killer-buyers started to lean forward like wolves eyeing their prey. She wasn't one I had come for, but she was one I went home with. Greasy Will actually dropped off bidding at $50, saying, "Let's let the lady have this one; she couldn't have any meat under that shaggy coat, anyway." He and the other regulars knew me, and we had worked out an uneasy peace between us. Occasionally their joking about tossing a bone to me meant one more horse for me to take home, so I would smile and quietly thank them for the "gift."

Of course, even in her heyday, Pretty Woman was never in danger of being called physically perfect. With her jug head, short thick neck, knock-knees, and disproportionate back, she would never win a beauty contest. But with a kind look in her eyes, the gentle way she held her head, and the relaxed expression of her mouth, she exuded warmth. In fact, Pretty Woman is one of the kindest mares I've ever had the good fortune to know. I would trust her implicitly with the hesitant balance of an unsteady child or with the fearfulness of the rankest amateur rider. No matter who it was or how badly they rode, she proudly carried each as if they were the most precious burden in the world. This is a horse that would come when called, running to the sound of her name. Scratch her behind the ears, and she was in ecstasy. It was surprising how very little it took to make her happy.

When it came time to find her a new home, I was very concerned that people would not be able to see past the homely exterior to the perfection of the interior. I knew what she was capable of, but how to express that to the average person? I carefully went down the list of potential adopters but, for one reason or another, none of them fit the bill. "Well, it won't break my heart to keep her around," I thought. "At least for a little longer, I can enjoy her company."

As fall faded into winter, it appeared Pretty Woman would stay at least until spring. Then my vet called and asked to send over someone whose elderly horse had been put to sleep; she also had a young horse sharing depression as they faced life without their beloved companion.

"I can vouch for her, Carol; she takes immaculate care of her horses. Please see if you have one for her," he pleaded.

Joanie came over to view the three I had available (I didn't count Pretty Woman on the list), but nothing clicked with them. Her eyes kept straying toward Pretty Woman who was, as usual, playing puppy on a leash next to me.

Joanie reached up and instinctively found the perfect place to scratch between the mare's ears. Eyes slotted in pleasure, Pretty Woman leaned into her hand.

"What about this one?" Joanie inquired.

"Well, she's not really pretty," I said, but before I could continue with "she is beautiful inside," Joanie interrupted me with, "Pretty is as pretty does."

Dumbstruck, I looked at her in amazement. I hadn't heard that expression since my grandmother passed away many years ago.

"And she does real pretty," I finally croaked out.

Pretty Woman has lived up to her name. She takes excellent care of the little gelding of Joanie's, and she coos and warbles to anyone who stops out into the field to visit with her. Scratch between her ears and she loves you for life, coo back at her and those soft eyes glow with love and pleasure. Pretty is as pretty does.

# *Enrichment Comes in Many Forms—Some with Legs*

The advantages to having a horse-enriched lifestyle fall into two categories—the obvious and the obtuse. Let's walk through a few and discuss them. Grab some coffee and pull that bucket over; get comfortable and relax. The obvious are relatively easy to recognize: riding, showing, companionship, and love, so we can spend this time talking about the more "hidden" benefits of being "owned" by horses.

First, you never have to get the weed whacker out to trim around your pool if you have horses. Dandelions, however, will still need pulling. Horses don't like them, either.

Running out of gas for the lawn mower halfway through cutting the front yard is no longer a worry. With a horse, you'll have an environmentally friendly lawn mower at your service. In addition, a horse will neatly deliver all-natural fertilization to selected areas.

There is a reason our ancestors stuffed sofas and pillows with horsehair. A horse can shed massive quantities of hair and fluff in the spring and fall. This is free padding from animal-friendly fur coats (whatever material your clothing was made of before you start grooming a shedding horse, it's all hair afterwards). It's also good insulation material and a great clearer of sinuses. A horse provides the raw material to plump pillows, reupholster living room sofas and chairs and make every bird's nest for miles around nice and comfy inside. All this goes for free—with nary a sneeze (at least, on the part of the horse), and it's a renewable resource; it comes back in record time to be shed again for your pleasure.

Horses have a way of keeping you on your toes—if for nothing else than to keep the horse's hooves off them. If you have a hammertoe, one application of horse hoof, firmly applied, resolves that nicely.

It's hard to get too fat or too out of shape with a horse around. If lugging around what has to go in one end (massive buckets of water, sixty-pound bales of hay, and fifty-pound bags of grain) doesn't keep your waistline trim, clearing up piles of what comes out the other end will.

The only sensation that comes close to the pleasure felt at arriving home from a hard day, getting out of the car, and being greeted by nickers and soft blows of welcome, is the one that derives from a similar greeting from your dog. And the only thing that tops it is to be greeted by horses and dogs simultaneously while unwinding a purring cat from around your ankles.

# *Horse Tales*

Here you go—could you just hold this lead line for me? His name? Well, that's Sterling Mixture—Mickey, for short—and he's a rare handful, isn't he? His mother was Lady, and unlike any of the others, hers was a planned pregnancy. All the other mares that gave birth here have come pregnant, with little or no prenatal care before they arrived. Just as in the human world, that means small, sickly babies, prone to every illness that comes around. We were certainly used to babies, but nothing prepared us for Sterling Mixture's arrival into the world. He even picked an appropriate date, Memorial Day, to be born. The night before Lady gave unmistakable signs that she would be foaling soon, and as she is my baby and this was her first baby, I settled into the barn with her to share her vigil.

It was a nice night outside, and the rest of the herd stayed out to enjoy the spring grass and give her some privacy. They seemed to know something was going on and kept coming up to the barn and peering in at us. Lady pawed her straw bedding around into a nice nest, then stepped over it and ignored it the rest of the night. She ate hay, yawned, drank water, groomed herself, and talked to me—in fact, she did everything but lie down and foal. Finally feeling foolish, I left the barn at 5 a.m. and went back to the house to lie down for awhile. My husband got up and went out to the barn thirty minutes later. He wasn't gone five minutes before he was back yelling, "You didn't tell me Lady had her baby, and I walked in on them."

"Impossible," I exclaimed, "I just left her, and she wasn't even showing signs of labor anymore."

"Well, she fooled you," he laughed. "You're a grandmother! Come see."

I ran out to be greeted by a complacent Lady and the longest-legged foal I had ever seen. "She must have wanted privacy," I muttered. "I wish she had told me and spared me a sleepless night."

I waited until after 9 a.m. to call my vet, and he came right out. He took one look toward the barn and laughed. Gathered outside one stall was the entire herd, peering through the boards and nickering.

"Guess I don't have to ask what stall they're in, do I?" My vet went up and looked in at Mickey, prancing around Lady, kicking his heels up, and just generally having a great time next to his exhausted mother.

"When was he born? He's that young and already so active? Better throw them both outside. He'll drive her crazy in here!"

His words proved prophetic. Mickey soon drove the whole herd crazy. Because he was the only baby, he was handled with indulgence, and he soon took great advantage of it. Poor Patches lost half his mane, and his tail looked as if it had been caught in a fence—all from Mickey chewing at it. No one—and nothing—was safe from the little terror except when he took a nap. We all—horses, sheep, dogs, cats, and humans—soon looked forward to Mickey's nap times. Woe betide anyone who woke him up early. The whole herd would tell them off. This brings us to the subject of Mickey's favorite place for his nap. Mickey would rest his head on the nice-cushioned back on my sheep. It would grow quiet, and we would look to find him taking his nap on the back of Stewart Lamb. The herd would sigh into sudden silence and give Stewart his orders: Move and wake up that baby and you'll die! A small defenseless lamb, Stewart took the orders seriously and stood quietly, acting as a pillow for hours at a time. The look in his eyes proclaimed, "Shush, don't wake the baby up now."

There is a wonderful story about Harry Houdini promising that if there were a life after death, he would come back and tell everyone. Well, I'm not sure about the rest of him, but his ability to perform magical escape feats certainly has returned in the person of Mickey. Oh, I'm sorry it is hard to visualize him when he's facing that way. Make a ninety-degree turn if you don't mind. I meant the horse, not you.

There, is that better? Yes, Mickey is now sixteen months old and, as you can tell from the downward slope, back end to front, he still has some growing to do. Thank you, he is turning out very handsome, but I must warn you he is also turning rapidly into the greatest escape artist that ever lived. Make sure you hang on to that lead line. I don't want to chase him into the woods again! Sorry, where was I? Oh yes, trying to tell you the tale of Mickey, the Sorcerer's Apprentice.

His mother, Lady, has always been able to open just about any lock I've attempted to keep her behind, and he seemed to absorb that information from birth. I can't tell you how many times he opened his stall and strolled out of the barn to investigate what the sheep were having for dinner. I finally thought I had resolved it when I latched both Dutch doors one evening, only to look up and find him waltzing down the aisle, a smug expression on his face. Confused, I went down to his stall to find the bottom door unlatched. He had opened it, laid down, and rolled on out.

When Mickey moved to my vet's for weaning, I truly did try and warn them about his propensity for letting himself out. Everyone stopped long enough from oohing and ahhing at his cute spots to nod blankly at me and remark that their stalls there were horse proof. I do believe (although they were too charitable to voice it) the thought crossed their minds that I was finally losing it and didn't know how to properly contain a youngster. I sighed and said, "Well, call me when he gets out. Everyone laughed at that, and I went home to console his mother over the absence of her trying offspring.

It takes about twenty minutes to get from my vet's office to The Last Refuge, and as I pulled up the driveway, I was met with the news that Mickey was loose in the woods behind the office, and could I call with suggestions for getting him to come back?

I immediately called and frantically asked how they could "lose" him in less than half an hour.

"We've captured the little bugger," was the sheepish response. "We'd no more than put him in the paddock, turned around, and he was out. Someone must have forgotten to lock the gate."

"More likely, he watched how it locked and unlocked it the same way," I returned.

"Carol, there isn't a horse alive that can unlock that gate," was the answer. "Okay," I said, "we'll see. And where is he now?"

"Safe and sound in his paddock, and I know it's locked. I did it myself," came sweetly back over the phone line.

I smiled to myself, thanked her, and as she was saying good-bye, I heard in the distance behind her the hysterical voice of one of her coworkers screaming, "Mickey's out again! Come help, quick!"

My vet has quite a few visitors stroll down to see his herd, and they always want to know why the poor baby's gate is chained and padlocked. I wonder how they explain that since anyone can see the regular lock is "horse proof"?

# *Doggone Tales*

My earliest memory is of my father trying to stand upright on the ice during a long, cold Nebraska winter. I remember seeing him come skating in the front door past a large dog who was carrying the Sunday roast in his mouth and trying to slink out the door, past my father.

One, two, or more dogs at a time have always owned members of my family. I am presently the happy property of five dogs: two Labs, a hound, a boxer, and one, a "wonder of modern genetic blending," who is called Beeper because of the sound he makes. I keep telling them the socially acceptable term is "guardian," but they insist they are unreconstructed, and if "own" was the term their Daddy used for his Person, then it's just plain good enough for them to use for me.

The following stories are about my relationship with that unbounded love wrapped in that hair-shedding skin and side-flinging saliva: the Dog.

# Quit Poking—I'm Typing

Chipper is leaping around me as I write this, poking at me with his nose and sweeping everything off the table with his sledgehammer tail. He is a chocolate Lab that thinks he's a horse (at horse feeding time), can imitate a cat (at cat feeding time), is The Dog (at dog feeding time), and masquerades as a human the rest of the time (people snack more than the others). He is also my best friend and has not only participated in nursing horses back to health, but has also raised cats, lambs, and baby chicks. He's demanding a pay raise as we speak.

My driveway runs six hundred feet back from the road, and Chipper rarely goes down it. There's too much to be done up here. One December morning, however, Chip insisted I get up at the horrendous hour of four a.m. (There is something inherent in the demands of a 100-pound Lab jumping on a water bed that makes "No, I'm not getting up" a futile statement). Chip doesn't bark; he woofles and pokes with his nose when he wants something. On this particular occasion, he punctuated his insistence by actually stealing my pillow from me and threatening to devour it. With that for a prod, down the dark driveway we went. Confronting me in the road at the base of the driveway was a paper bag, mewing and moving. Chip ran to the bag, carefully picked it up and brought it to me. Inside were two tiny kittens and more fleas than I'd seen on a grown animal, much less on babies too young to open their eyes.

Chip pushed me back toward the house and warmth. I washed the filth from the kittens and was going to place them next to the wood stove while I fixed some formula for them, but Chip took each one tenderly in his mouth and carried it to his bed. He lay down and tucked them under him for warmth. The only way I could feed them was to get on the floor next to Chip's bed and nurse them there. He wasn't letting them out of his sight. For the next four months, we raised kittens together. Chip would keep his eye on them and, if they got in mischief, he would pick them up by the scruff of the neck and carry them back to their bed.

Both Marvin and Millie have grown into beautiful cats that have a strange fixation for liking to be carried around in a dog's mouth. They will come up to be groomed by Chip, and then he will pick one up and carry it around, while the other one chases him. They gave the meter reader quite a start the other day!

One of Chip's other favorite hobbies is the same as mine: taking care of the horse herd. He just loves being out with them and, if they put their heads down, he grooms their faces for them. The Last Refuge is a pampering place. The horses all love this; it's just that when Chip gets carried away and demands carrots and grain, they will put their foot down and gently move him away. When he gets hold of a carrot, he plays catch with the whole herd chasing him. Usually he makes it all the way across the field and back under the fence, where I am faced with grabbing a slimy carrot and tossing it back before Lady comes over after it.

Chipper has lots more stories he considers it's important I tell you, but right now, he is demanding a dog biscuit (poke, poke, poke). I'll be back later with more.

# *Diet? Do You Want Me to Die?*

I really should put a picture on this page of Topaz's graduation day. In glorious color, you might have been able to see him and his new owner getting back from a ride. TJ and Chip and I were there to greet him and give our final stamp of approval to the new bond. I was mentally composing the fluent turns of speech, the allegories that would have made you weep for the poetry of my phrases. As I said, it's a wonderful story full of triumphs and a perfect ending. Unfortunately, you're not going to hear it here. A crisis of monumental proportions has developed at The Last Refuge. How monumental? Chip topped 105 pounds on the vet's scale yesterday. There is no longer any choice. We are dieting.

When I told Chipper this was it, he threw a fit. Upon hearing I was going to tell the world (put the news out in a story so he can't cheat and cadge biscuits from you while I'm not looking), he chewed up every picture of himself he could find. That's why Topaz's graduation story will have to wait. It had the only current picture of Chipper that was left in one piece until the Chip Dog found it and ate it too. I had to stop writing that award-winning story to address this issue. I just had to get the alert out before he commandeered the computer tonight and sent his plea for biscuits out to the net. No matter what you hear, do not send any biscuits to us until further notice, please.

**OUCH! Don't! Let go of my ponytail! Help me! I'm being dragged away by ...RRRR!**

Growl...what is this nonsense typed above? Anyone could tell from that picture (before I ate it) that the porky one, the one needing the diet is *not* I. Don't know why Carol would tell such lies. Usually, she's a pretty good pet. I know she's not perfect—still climbs into bed without asking, and her table manners—well, I cannot for the life of me break her from wanting to eat what's on her plate instead of giving it to me. But for all that, I've always known I could depend on her. Until this insane idea that I need to be on a diet crept into her pea brain, I always thought we were real pals. Well, the fact of the matter is, *she* should diet and give me all her food! What's that noise? Oh no, the vet is at the door and he looks mad! Let go of that phone, Carol. Okay now, wait here, you all, and I'll be right back!

There I wasn't gone long, now was I? I've got the vet and Carol held hostage, and if you ever want to hear from either of them again, you will send biscuits, bones, and gravy to my e-mail address. Otherwise, they can just diet together in the closet, and I have at least three days worth of food in the refrigerator and cupboard before I have to let them out. Darn! Does anyone out there know how to operate a can opener?

# *Doggone Daze*

Hi there again! While I'm finishing up my latest story about Chipper's diet, grab a hay bale and sit down, I'll be right with you.

Chip has been fairly good-natured about his diet the last six weeks. We had a scare here when he raided the storage area in the garage for horse grain and tried to burst his stomach from gorging, but that is past, and he's appeared to settle down a bit and is more accepting of the program.

Chipper has gotten a lot of email recently from people who are under the impression his name is Chocolate Chip because of his color. He has demanded I explain his real name is "Summerset's Chip Off the Old Block," and he acquired that name by looking exactly like his dad's baby pictures when he was six weeks old. His father, Longmeadow's Herschel's Discovery, may be up at the Rainbow Bridge, but his legacy lives on through his children. Of the nine in the one litter that Hersch fathered, eight made champion. Only one didn't and that was, you guessed it, our illustrious, bone-loving, good-natured "foster anything and love it" dog. He flunked puppy kindergarten! I've never before had a dog that was too interested in what was going on around him to bother with passing puppy kindergarten. But then again, there's never been another dog like him anywhere.

I know, everyone thinks their dog is unique and, of course, they all are. But Chip has a few quirks that surpass unique and border on being baroque. I'm going to grab a quick cup of coffee and share a few with you. You might want to get a glass of something, as well. It does make the laughter flow smoother.

Sunday night is warm mash night here for the horses. It steams away all day and they get more and more anxious as the afternoon wears on, pacing the fence and calling for dinner from about 2 p.m. on. Right next to them is Chipper, egging them on and doing a few low calls of his own. When the mash is served up, he's right there, demanding his own serving of it. Since the start of his diet, his portion has been just a taste, but that doesn't prevent him from going into Lady's stall, rearing up on his hind legs and burying his muzzle into her feed bin, next to her, and helping her eat! Any other dog (or horse, as she's the alpha mare here) would be kicked out over the divider, if not through it. But not Chipper. She pokes him away with her nose, and he just comes back. Lady will sigh, make room for him, and when the mash is done, complain to me about how he got the lion's share. I've repeatedly told her not to put up with it, but that's her "Chipper-dad" (he helped raise her), and she won't stand up to him. The sight of more than 1400 pounds of horse backing off from 89 pounds (yes, in spite of the mash, we are losing weight) of dog is amazing since he does it by gentle persuasion rather than with teeth and growls.

Whenever anyone comes to visit, they soon learn that they have to be very careful when they go to leave. Chipper will jump into any and all open car doors and immediately assume what he considers his rightful place, behind the steering wheel. That's all right with friends, but he has startled a few UPS drivers. He just loves to go "bye-bye," and all my recent vehicle purchases have revolved around whether Chip would be comfortable in the proposed buy or not. I can tell you for a fact that he doesn't fit in a two-door compact, and they make the back seats of Saturns out of some kind of tasty material. Currently, a Crew Cab Ford Pickup has worked out great except for the unmentionable day Chip crawled between me and the steering wheel on the interstate, got stuck, and we could only go straight. There was no room to turn the wheel. We had to wait till there was no traffic, then glide to a stop, and as I was trying to peel him out so I could breath and we could continue, a state trooper (fortunately, with a love for dogs and a sense of humor) screeched to a halt behind me, came charging up, looked in the window and burst into laughter. He said from behind, all he could see was a dark brown dog's head, and, for one frozen moment, he thought Chipper was driving. He said he was glad to see there was someone squished in behind Chipper as he wasn't sure how he was going to write up a ticket for a Lab! I was glad to see him, too, as it took him pulling, me shoving, and Chip grunting to extricate us. The warning (failure to maintain control of vehicle due to dog behind steering wheel) was the trooper's way of proving to his pals back at the barracks what had happened, and I'm sure he gained himself a few laughs.

When the phone rings here, Chipper is always the first to get to it, and if I'm not fast enough, he has it off the hook and is snuffling at it. That's my fault. I've always encouraged him to listen on the phone to my mother and some of my friends when they call, as he recognizes voices over the phone and wuffles back at them. Chip's just taken it one step further and doesn't wait to be invited. I've run for the phone and found it on the ground, Chip wuffling at it, and some confused person on the other end plaintively repeating, "Is your mother there? Get your mother, now!"

Usually I just say nothing about who answered the phone if it's a stranger. My friends all know, and it's just too hard to explain to a stranger that I have a dog that insists on taking messages. It's bad enough having to explain why Chip and I were singing once in the shower together to a repairman who came in unexpectedly from outside and heard us. But that's a story I'm not going to try and talk my way out of here—suffice to say, I sing in the shower and Chip just loves to be wherever I am.

Well, it's getting late and I have chores to do. Chip is tugging at my leg and poking me with reminders that Lady is bugling the dinner bell outside. Enjoy the rest of your visit at The Last Refuge and come back soon. Oh, and Chip says to be sure and bring him a bickie and leave it in his round bed. He also has his own email address so you can mail them to him if you don't have time to stop. He's considerate that way; he doesn't want to put you out. And if you do stop by, please check your car carefully on the way out. He blends in well with a shadowy interior, and I'd hate to see you meet that state trooper on your drive out, the way I did.

# *You Did It Now, Chip*

Let's see...awhile back when we talked (grab some more coffee, and there should be cookies unless Chip gobbled them all again), I started to tell you about the chicken incident. Well it all started, as do most tales here, in the barn. It was getting on toward spring, and we were discussing what we should plant for a garden. We had quite a lively discussion going on about the merits of various types of corn, potatoes, and so forth, until the recurring theme of "bug control" reared its ugly head. A friend of mine pointed out that chickens are great controllers of the critters, and they would reduce the risk of having to use non-natural pesticides. I thought about that, and the luxury of having fresh eggs sounded like a real winner, so I called my favorite feed store to order baby chicks and all the equipment. They said there was a special going and would deliver a couple of dozen the next week. I told Chip all about it, and though he looked skeptical, he was appeased when I reminded him that these would be animals that didn't like dog biscuits.

Came delivery day and the truck driver started unloading my order:

- 50 bags of grain, check.
- 2 boxes of dog food, check.
- 25 pounds of dog biscuits, check. Leave them alone, Chip!
- 4 salt licks, check.
- 1 bag Grow Chick Feed, check.
- 1 Grow-Light, check
- 1 box eggs...Oh, no! Where are my baby chicks?

Don't you laugh at me. What am I going to do with eggs? Hatch them? How? I will not! They'll break!

I made a quick trip to the feed store (why do all men have to laugh and offer the same suggestion on how to hatch eggs?), and one *expensive* incubator later, the eggs were installed and ready to hatch into chickens. (At this rate, I was going to have the most un-cost effective eggs in the world.)

Chip was so interested in this new piece of equipment and its contents (he loves eggs), that he had his big nose in investigating any time the top was opened. Every day we turned eggs and looked for signs of life. Finally came the big day (of course, Chip was first to notice and was right there, nose and all), and the eggs began rocking and cracking.

Well, yes, I did remember Konrad Lorenz-Somebody had done a study on bird imprinting, but that wasn't the first thing on my mind at that moment. And whether Chip had ever heard of such a thing—well, who can tell? The fact of the matter is, the initial sight those baby chicks had at birth was Chip and his nose! Their first sound was his soft wuffling (I was too awestruck to speak). And of course, that was it for those chicks: Here was Mama!

Now, I know it's natural for baby chicks to follow their mother everywhere, and it was cute to see them do that to Chip, but did he have to pick them up and put them in my bed? Have you ever tried to housebreak a chicken? Or tried to convince them that their place is outside laying expensive eggs, not inside cheep-wuffling for dog biscuits? Thank goodness, Chip isn't a barker and doesn't chase the mailman. Can you imagine those chickens imitating that behavior?

Eggs? Well, yes, those chickens did finally grow up and start laying, but Chip thinks they're his grandchildren, so how can I do that to him? Anyone want some eggs, cheap? We have trouble eating them here. Quit poking, Chip, I'm kidding. I like sleeping with the birds!

# Doggone Truths

This is the Chipper Dog here. I am The Dog. See me type. I've decided that this barn chat area is a good place to tell you about what really goes on here at The Last Refuge. Mom usually tries to keep me and my opinions locked up on the other side of the book. She thought for sure I was busy with the chickens, but I've escaped and decided to come visit you here in the barn.

First off, The Last Refuge is a giant playground for dogs; the horses are just here for my convenience. Quit gasping. It is not rank insubordination. Give a feller a chance to explain, will ya? I care as much about my horse buddies as any dog ever could. Sheesh, who else could nuzzle me half as well? And they always share their grain and carrots with me. In fact, life without horses would be just plain boring, and that doesn't even get into being able to always have someone to play tag with, or splash in the pond with.

Now that it is clear how much I love my horses, let me explain about convenience. When things happen around here (which can be daily), it is convenient to be able to look innocent, shake my head, and sorrowfully exclaim, "The horses did it."

For instance:

Someone broke into the closet and took the garbage can out, emptied it, and buried the remains under Mom's bed. Who we going to blame?

Someone dug a trench through the remains of the herb garden. Who we going to blame?

Someone played tug of war with the pantyhose that were "peeking" out of a half-opened drawer. Who we going to blame?

Someone drank all the water out of that white "water bowl" in the bathroom and then kissed Mom hello. Who we going to blame?

Someone caught a frog and laid it out proudly on Mom's bed. Who we going to blame?

Someone rolled in the mud and rubbed it off on the couch. Who we going to blame?

Someone broke the Z-key on the typewriter testing it out with a paw (er, hoof). Who we going to blame?

Someone dragged all the clothes off the line and spread them out in the mud. Who we going to blame?

Someone ate all the cat's food. Who we going to blame?

Someone wrote all these things about why horses are a dog's convenience. Who we going to blame?

# *Hard Choices and No Easy Answers*

This is the story of how it can be both a sunset and a sunrise—simultaneously. It is also, and more important, the story of a man and a woman and their love for a dog. Almost seven years ago, a litter of chocolate Labs was born at a kennel and advertised for sale. One of those puppies went home with a man and his wife. This is their story, one of the most unselfish love stories I've ever witnessed.

Bailer went home with the man and his wife, and the young marriage and the young dog grew up together. He was their first-born son and very dearly cherished. His dad would rush home to be greeted ecstatically by body-wagging, Lab-grinning joy. His mom fretted over his frequent ear infections and tenderly concocted tasty morsels to tempt his appetite. Weekends were devoted to playing with Bailer, enjoying each other and their loving companion. Wherever the man went, leaning against him and loving him with those limpid Lab eyes was Bailer.

Times change, marriages grow, and a little one was born to Bailer's two-legged parents. Bailer was excited and tenderly protective of his new sister. He was her leaning post for her first steps, a warm rug for toddler naps, drier of tears, and sharer of joy. The family's happiness was complete, and integral to the love was the Lab. A little grayer, a little frayed around the ears, but still so generous with his love, Bailer completed the circle.

As the little one grew, lifestyles changed and so did the family's address. Gone was the large yard to romp in. Gone were the dear ones during the long days. Gone was the freedom to play. The dog was alone. Bailer was confused, upset, and so very, very sad. He cried, and he howled his despair and tore at his ears in his agony. The man and his wife were distraught. Bailer, their beloved dog, was heartsick and they had no cure. If they left him inside, he tore through the house; if they left him outside, he screamed. Remedy after useless remedy was attempted with no abatement of Bailer's pain. Finally the dreaded truth was faced: Bailer needed more than they could give him. Bailer needed others; he cried out for companionship they could no longer provide. In short, to give Bailer what love demanded, love demanded they give Bailer up.

There is no knife edge keen enough, no scalpel sharp enough, to cut as deeply as that decision sliced into the family. The power to love is the power to hurt, and there was infinite love in the man and his wife, which translated to mind-numbing, breath-stealing pain. What Bailer needed they would give him, but could they ever smile easily again, knowing and remembering? Minds made up, with shaking hands and tentative voices, they began their search for a new home for Bailer. They carefully listed the requirements. It would have to be in the country, with a large yard, and, oh yes, other animals, and children, and someone who would stay home with him. Most important, Bailer would need to like the people, and they would have to love him. The dream grew and the search went on.

With deep humility and a sense of awe, I am proud to tell you The Last Refuge was selected as Bailer's new home. Thanksgiving came twice that year. The second occasion was the Saturday after the first, and it arrived the day Bailer came to stay. I watched this man and his wife look around at the land, tearfully smile at Bailer's ecstatic play with his long-put-away ball, the dog's joyous leap into the pond, and his eyes as he ran and tumbled with Chipper. I saw them gulp back tears, clutch each other's hands in their misery, and I heard their offer of their first-born. Tears streamed down my face, and I hurt for their pain as I accepted.

Sunrise slowly slipped into sunset and back again. Somewhere in time, their marriage is new and Bailer is a puppy. Just over that horizon, they are playing in the sun, and we are on this side. Like two sides to the same coin, we dance together in celebration of the love we share for a dog, Bailer. He is theirs and he is ours, and the love washes through and within him. Bailer wags his body in overall joy, and the people he has brought together glorify in that happiness.

# Short Tales from Times Gone By

Going through my collection of stories and dividing them into logical groupings—horses here, dogs there (Drop that. It's not edible, Chip) left me with a small pile of stories that kept struggling out of the easily labeled areas and just sort of setting there on their own merits, smiling at me. It's great they have such self-confidence in their own worth, but classifying them escapes me.

As close as I can come is to say, "This is where I came from." No, that's not quite right. Let me try again: "These stories illustrate other facets of my mentality." No. Too grandiose and pretentious. Plus it makes me feel like a snob, and being dressed in barn clothes with horse scum embedded under my nails does not a snob make. Okay, enough dithering: "Here is another collection of stories; you classify them, please." Now that works! Pass the cookie plate and don't hog all the oatmeal ones, Chip.

# *My Mother Is an Artist*

New visitors to my home invariably stop and admire the pictures on my walls. The seascapes beckon one to shed shoes and adulthood, to bury one's toes in the crystal sand and frolic in the waves. Landscapes shimmer with sunbeams weaving an intricate pattern through the leaf-tossed shadows. The bowl of fruit displayed on my dining room wall begs one to caress the fuzzed bloom of the peach, inhale the fragrance of the grapes, grab hold of an apple and savor its crisp sensation. My walls resonate with life, love, family, and harmony to appreciative senses. When the enraptured viewer asks how I got such wonderful paintings, I proudly explain, "My mother is an artist."

My mother may have painted when she was young, but the raising of five children allowed no time for "hobbies." She only recently took back up the brush and began creating. I used to think what a shame it was that she hadn't kept up the painting through all those years of child raising. What masterpieces had been lost within her unfulfilled dreams of that time? Yet, watching my mother interact with her grandson caught me up short, tumbling my memory through cascading pictures of my childhood. Smiles and tears flowed as I remembered.

My mother is an artist. She paints with glowing colors on canvas now, but when I was young, her canvas was the five new lives God had entrusted her with—and her paints...oh, the glory and splendor of the color palette she used!

**Coral Red.** It was the first color to be deeply etched in the depths of our beings. Coral Red, Love Red, Sure Red. There was no doubt, no ambiguity about her brush strokes here. We each knew with every fiber of our being that we had been wanted, we were loved, and we would always be loved.

**Sunshine Yellow.** Her happiness welled up and flowed though us, lighting our existence, and warming our way. Her glance, touch, smile, words, and gestures radiated solar warmth that banished shadows and tinted our subconscious with the realization that happiness is from within, a well that must be shared lest it go prematurely dry—a life-giving source available to all and denied to none of God's creations. She painted its route for us.

**Constancy Green.** My mother has always been there for us; she is the heart of my family to this day. Constant and unwavering, no matter what I had done, the gentle wisp of this color still shone through the black of my disgrace. I hear her in my mind when I want to give up on something. Green feathers brush my mental vision, and strength flows through her to me.

**Silver Piety.** She was generous with this color and lavished it thickly on five protesting (I don't want to go to church, Mom) children. I thought for a few years the color had leeched out, but instead, it had bided its time and when needed, it blazed out, lifting me upward to see what she had offered so long ago. God's glory and His existence were there, and the paint was still silver bright.

**Tea Rose, Peach Rose Petal.** Soft powder clouds of color, a love for animals and appreciation of God's gift of life, and wells of joy all flowed through my mother's touch. Her bright gaze draws animals to her; her reverent appreciation of them sparks answering emotions. She tinted my life with this love, and it gushes forth fountains of pink, yellow, red, and blush.

**Royal Blue Duty and Honor.** Splashes of blue dot my horizons. Life choices are bound within this framework. She always anchored my questions, self-doubts, and my ability to make rational decisions to two sturdy bastions of blue strength—duty and honor. They've never failed me, and sometimes when I look into a mirror, their blue shines back at me from behind my eyes, and I thank God for my mother.

My mother is an artist. She paints with glowing colors on canvas now, but the palette she used for her earlier works reverberates through my soul, and the texture of her strokes defines and uplifts my existence.

# Casual Acts of Kindness

Driving home one evening on the interstate, I came over a hill to face a fairly common sight: A car was pulled over into the breakdown lane with its hood up. Standing next to it was a distressed, distraught, very pregnant woman, and hanging out of car windows were enough little girls to stock a brownie troop. It was "going home time," and drivers were whizzing by, oblivious to all except the call of home. Although no mechanic, I pulled over in front of her and stopped. If nothing else, I could relay a message for her to get someone to fix the problem. As I opened the truck door and stepped out, a car full of teenage boys with wild hair, earrings, and rather obscene slogans on their shirts slammed to a stop behind her, and they all poured out in a loud, gangly heap. She froze and had the look of a headlight-caught deer in her eyes. I practically ran to get next to her before the gang could reach the car and its defenseless cargo.

The tableau was set. On one side, a gray-haired older woman, a pregnant younger one, and five young girls all facing six hulking youths in what looked like gang jackets. The silence shut down the world around us and narrowed our existence to an infinite awareness of the players in our little circle. Instinctively, the young mother's hand reached out for mine as the gang drew level with the car. The leader of the group looked at his followers spread in a semi-circle behind him, smiled at us and said, "Can we help? This is no place for a couple of women and children to be stranded. I wouldn't want my mother to be waiting on the side of the road like this." The boisterous herd of males surged toward the stricken car, flowed over the engine, and, with incredible skill, had it running in no time. After making sure all was well and refusing payment, they wished us a good night and departed. She and I shared a smile, got in our respective vehicles and went our ways. I wonder if any of those young men even told their parents what they did, or was it just a casual act of kindness to them?

I have a blind horse here at The Last Refuge. His eyesight left him gently and so slowly that we all hoped he could adapt as it faded. The hardest thing for him was the walk to the pasture in the morning and the return to the barn in the evening. At first, I used to halter and lead him slowly out, release the halter, and leave him next to the pond on the succulent grass for the day. In the evening, I would halter and lead him back. He seemed very discouraged that the others moved off ahead of him, freely making the trip in front of us. Even extra whispered words of endearment and caresses couldn't make up for the loss of his independence, and he was showing signs of depression. This was serious, for a horse that cannot adapt is a horse that will not survive. The rest of the herd will shun a depressed horse, and the loneliness saps their will to live.

Just before I was willing to admit the situation was getting critical, a new and very timid mare arrived here. Madel came off the racetrack, had never been given free socialization time with other horses, and our herd terrified her. The first few days she was out with them, she held back next to the front fence and looked forlornly over it at the barn. I am sure she was counting the minutes until she could return to the safety of her stall. Then one morning, as I was leading my poor old blind baby out, Madel came along the other side and walked with us to the pond. She nuzzled him, and when he was freed, walked off next to him, where he was grazing.

I smiled and thought, "If anyone needed someone, it was those two." Each time I checked the field during that day, they were together.

As five o'clock came, I went into the barn to get the halter and lead line. I could hear the herd approaching and opened the side door to let them in and get settled. I could then go get my blind one in peace. The herd came in, Madel hanging way back as usual. In the approaching dusk, her silhouette looked strange as she came toward the lighted area in front of the barn. I looked, blinked, and looked again. Carefully, slowly, with soft-mouthed patience, she was approaching and, with his nose over her back, came her blind friend. He stopped when she did, turned with her, and they moved as one. Into the barn happily he came, led by his newfound friend. Both horses looked proud—she for her friend, and he for his independence of the hated halter. I wiped my tear-filled eyes and wondered if she truly realized the gift she was giving him or whether it was a casual act of kindness on her part?

# *Riding the Bus*

When I was a junior in high school (a thousand years ago), I was able to be involved in a Westinghouse Summer Intern Program that, although an exciting experience, meant I got up each morning at 4 a.m. and rode an incredibly crowded bus for two hours into the city to be in the program. There were a lot of regulars on the bus, more than there were seats for, and we daily jostled one another in order to sit part of the way. Every evening, I repeated the bus ride back, getting home at 7 p.m., helping my mother with chores, studying, doing homework, and finally getting to bed by midnight. Towards the end of the summer, I used to really look forward to the bus ride home on Fridays. I could sleep until 6 a.m. the next two days and take it a bit easier.

One Friday evening, I was really tired and got on the bus to face the last seat open, and I gratefully fell in it. At the next stop, several people, including an elderly woman I had seen on the bus almost daily, got on and everyone on the bus knew there were no more stops for an hour, and anyone getting up to offer their seat would stand for that hour. As the crowd shuffled on the bus and reached up to grab the handrails, this woman moved in front of me and sighed. I have never wanted so bad to look down at my feet and stay where I was in my life (I have a sad smile remembering that internal torment). For a brief moment, I was tied to the seat, and then I stood up and moved out of the way for her. She looked surprised, grateful, and then sat down. She insisted on holding my books for me and, for the next hour, I stood and swayed in front of her till we hit the next stop. After more passengers disembarked, I was able to sit down next to her for the last hour of the trip.

She talked with me and somehow it came out she was heading back from the VA hospital, where her husband of fifty-one years lay dying. She had no children; she had outlived her sisters and brothers, and she was facing this daily trip to visit him alone with only her memories. I remember how very swollen and red her knuckles were and how lined and tired her face was.

I can still close my eyes and smell the scent of the violet perfume she wore and how she said it was her husband's favorite. For that next hour, I breathed in that scent and felt her sad joy as she talked about the life she had shared with her beloved husband. I sat mesmerized by all she shared with me and humbled by the gift of that conversation. As we reached her stop, she turned to me and said, "Thank you for being there on the bus with me. It's hard to travel it alone." I never saw her again and do not know if that meant her husband died or something else had happened. I used to fantasize that he had miraculously gotten cured over that weekend and she had taken him home, and they were happy again together.

    I consider that bus ride a watershed moment in my life. I promised myself that no one will ever ride a bus alone if I am around. That is the gift that woman gave to me and I try to share with everyone else I meet.

# *Time*

That time is relative seems to be one of those simple statements of fact that we have all heard and ignored for years. Sometimes we are pulled up short when graphic descriptions of it confront us; the rest of the time, we just flow with it. When I was a teenager and going through that "dark, melancholy" phase between fourteen and wisdom, I wrote a poem about time, the only part of which I still remember being this refrain:

> The Present becomes the past,
> The Future never arrives.
> Man now is in the present,
> But now to yesterday dies.

*I did warn you this was written during that stage of approaching adulthood where all my clothes were black, didn't I?*

I have a minute or so to spare, so I thought we could play a game. Let's take the phrase "Just a minute, please" and describe the circumstances under which it is verbalized or otherwise expressed and compute the relative length of time within each context by the speaker and listener. Ready?

**"Just a minute, please.":** spoken by children to parents on being asked when they are going to (1) start their homework, or (2) clean their room, or (3) take out the garbage, or (4) _____ fill in the blank. **Parents:** That phrase had better mean *now*). **Children:** Sometime...tonight, maybe.

**"Just a minute, please.":** irritably uttered by a frazzled parent to a child that has just asked for the hundredth time, "When are we going to get there?" from the back seat of a too-small car. **Child:** That had better be in this lifetime already. **Parent:** Sixty seconds from now, you will be walking if you don't keep quiet!

**"Just a minute, please.":** muttered to a dog violently asking to go outside by its owner, who just wants to sleep a little longer. **Owner:** It's only 5 a.m. Please let me sleep till 6. **Dog:** If that squirrel on the back deck gets away, your slippers are in big trouble.

**"Just a minute, please.":** expressed by the vacant gaze and nonchalant air of a dog that does not want to come back when called. **Dog:** I can't tell time anyway, so how much can you scold me if I wag my tail? **Owner:** Don't you pretend not to have heard me. Now means *now*.

**"Just a minute, please.":** a horse owner's plea to a horse kicking at the stall door in a frenzy to go out and eat new spring grass. **Owner:** Just let me get a few more tangles out of that mane of yours and one more nose kiss in before you go out and roll. **Horse:** Did I tell you that I've figured out how to cow kick?

**"Just a minute, please.":** a chat room addict to spouse when asked for the fifth time if they're ever coming to bed. **Addict:** I'm coming...oh, look at what that one just wrote. **Spouse:** Only a snore; the spouse gave up and went to bed two hours ago.

**"Just a minute, please.":** A busy waitress to a very vocal customer who is staring forlornly into an empty coffee cup. **Customer:** It's been empty so long, the cup has dried out. **Waitress:** In your dreams, Bud. The last time you were here, you left me only a fifty-cent tip.

**"Just a minute, please.":** An announcer reading the winning lottery numbers and pausing before the final number. **Listener No. 1**, who thinks he's got the first numbers all correct but can't find the actual ticket to check: Wait, wait! Not so fast, please. **Listener No. 2**, who has his ticket and knows he's got all the numbers correct so far: Well, come on already! How long do you think I can hold my breath? **Listener No. 3**, with no numbers right on his ticket so far: He isn't even in front of the TV any longer; he's off in the kitchen grabbing a snack. **Announcer:** I guess they've squirmed enough. The last number is...

**"Just a minute, please.":** Owner to cat winding around her legs with cries for food. **Owner:** I fed you an hour ago. How can you be starving again already? Where is that can opener? **Cat:** Just because I have nine lives doesn't mean I want to waste one on dying of hunger. The can opener is right there. Let me push you in the right direction.

**"Just a minute please.":** Counting down...sixty, fifty-nine, fifty-eight, fifty-seven...one. There that didn't take too long, did it? Did it? Where did everyone go? I took only a minute or so.

# *Sometimes I Remember and Smile*

It has become increasingly apparent to me that each of us holds a small, secret place within where we store our treasures. These can include memories that suddenly erupt and toss us backwards through the ebb tide pools of time to emerge in another where, another when. The taste of ice cream, a snatch of song, a particular phrase—anything can trigger this occurrence. And as the days between my emergence into this world march more distantly than the days till my exit, the memories come faster and sharper, echoing the past in painfully sweet nostalgia. Such a whirlpool occurred to me this week. I was driving home and saw a postman who had stopped and was talking with a woman getting her mail. Suddenly floodgates in my mind opened, and memories poured through of the greatest love story I have ever known.

It was post-World War II and many Americans were gearing up for the new era that was rising. Men who were back from the wars were reuniting with families and making up for lost time. My father was just such a home-again soldier, going to school on the GI Bill and working as a postman to fill the gaps in his wallet. He was delivering mail in Mill Valley (at the time, a small town across from San Francisco) on a hot summer's day and was stopped on the street by a tiny woman with the Philadelphia habit of rolling her *r*'s. She introduced herself as the new tenant of the house and explained that her husband, a navy doctor, had just been transferred out there. Upon my father saying he had just got out of the military, she asked a few questions (casually inquiring about his marital status along the way) and, finding he was single, said, "Come back after you finish delivering the mail. I have cold root beer and three daughters."

As he loved to tell the story, it was a very hot day, and he could always elude the daughters, so he accepted. When he came back, he was introduced to them, and before he left, he had asked my Aunt Carol to go swimming with him the next weekend. He also turned to my mother and said she could tag along if she wanted; he had a friend named Frank whom he'd invite to make it a foursome. By the end of that date, my mother was with my father, and Aunt Carol with

Uncle Frank. Before the month was out, both daughters were engaged and the weddings occurred within a year. My grandmother was fond of saying it was the best root beer she ever served—two daughters married for the price of one bottle.

They were married in 1948 and happily had—and raised—five children. Over the course of the next forty-seven years, they shared laughter, tears, humor, and sadness. Each was the other's best friend and until the day he died, I never saw my father look at my mother without the light of love in his eyes. My mother would look back at him, and the shared emotions between them would warm any room they were in. Their house was always full of kids, animals, and the smells of fresh baked goodies. And the humor! There was always humor. There was nothing was so awful it couldn't be laughed about.

I remember my father taking us out for a Sunday ride, deliberately speeding up and down hills, hitting the bottom with such force we all bounced, and he'd laugh and say, "Oops, my lady."

My mother would say, "Careful, Bill," and he'd laugh and break into song. We kids would egg him on to greater speeds (at least 35 miles an hour, as I look back), and my mother would sigh, pat his hand, and then join in the song.

Money could be tight at times, and there were days where the big treat was three Popsicles that could be brought home and carefully split to make six. Counting my parents, there were seven of us, and they always made a joke out of which one of them really didn't like Popsicles. The funny thing about that is, as I remember now, it sure seems as if they took turns being the one who "hates Popsicles, no thank you," and they'd laugh.

My father had this dead-pan expression he could put on when he was pulling "a good one" that sucked you right in and dragged you under before you saw the punch line. I can't tell you how many people he told that there were four years difference between him and my mother, and we kids were hers by her first marriage. He had them believing he was the "young" man who had married an "older woman with kids." Never mind that all five of us were carbon copies of him and, when seen with him, there was no denying our parentage. He'd just glibly say, "Well, I've known her for awhile," and laugh.

I can't eat a Baby Ruth candy bar to this day without seeing my father carefully folding the wrapper, turning to me and asking, "Have you ever had one of these before?" Upon my answering "No," he displayed the folded name reduced down to Bath and said, "Well, don't you think you should?"

My mother was no slouch either when it came to thinking fast. I can remember proudly standing on the back step, knocking at the door with a large snake dangling from my fist. She opened the door, saw the snake, rapidly shut the door, and called through it, "If you're not bitten, dinner will be ready in ten minutes. Let it go and come in." It wasn't until years later I found out she was terrified of snakes and it was all she could do to not scream at the sight of one of her children in the "grasp of a serpent."

The best memories, though, are of the two of them together. They could ballroom dance beautifully, flowing together and around each other to the ebb and tide of the music. My father would tenderly enfold my mother, and they would dip and sway, spin and whirl, as if there was one mind uniting the two bodies. There was certainly one heart, beating in two chests, but in perfect harmony. When a child-rearing decision needed to be reached, they would look at each other, and in the wordless communion of perfect union, come to a consensus, then turn to the waiting child and declare the answer. There was never a chance to divide and conquer in our household, as much as I now shamefacedly admit that, on occasion, we tried.

There were so many animals waiting to greet my father as he approached the Rainbow Bridge, I envision St. Peter having to open both gates to let the crowd in. And I know that as soon as he had them all settled in their new home, he sat down and taught them to harmonize with his songs. Sometimes I close my eyes, and I can hear his laughter and feel his touch. My soul vibrates to the sound of his wonderful tenor as he fills the heavens with his stories and his joy. Although they are physically apart, I look into my mother's eyes and my father winks back at me. And sometimes, like this week, a sight, or a sound brings the memories tumbling back, and I smile and thank God for my parents. This is the Greatest Love Story I have ever known, and it keeps me warm in the cold, bleak times of my life.

# *Poetry in Motion*

Heroes are the subject of many a rousing story told through the years. From our earliest ancestors, entertaining small children around an evening fire with the tale of how their uncle saved everyone in the tribe from a bear, through the Greek sagas of the Trojan wars, Beowulf's heroism in Anglo-Saxon times, and Saint George's slaying the dragon in an era now mythic, our past been gilded in the reflected glow of the glory that is called Hero. My father, a hero in his own right, once told me the difference between a hero and a coward is the direction they run when faced with immense peril and heart-stopping fear. I looked at him and laughed, thinking in my naiveté that only a hero would use that for an excuse.

Over the decades, I've heard of several heroes, and I have had the good fortune to stand next to a few of them, my head bowed and my face rosy-cheeked from the wonder of being so close to the doer of such valiant deeds. All of them exude life in crackling energy, barely contained within their skin. Each fiercely loves what they protect, whether it is an idea, a person, a concept, or an animal. Heroes do not pick the direction they run in. They are propelled by feelings, compelled by intellect, and repelled by evil. Heroes must; cowards will not.

Somewhere in this world, a horse cries in abject fear, shakes uncontrollably as it faces the smell of blood, the finality of existence. The uncaring around him do not stop to comfort or offer support; his pain does not impinge on their awareness.

In Spain, a young hero clenches his pen painfully, and tears roll unheeded down his cheeks as the horse's cries flow through the inner part of his soul. Our hero hears, our hero suffers, our hero stands and shakes his fist and says, "No more!" He slowly counts his hard-earned money—this much for rent, for school, for food. Sighing, he reaches into the fund for food and pulls out half of it. This much for phone calls to stop the cries, this much for faxes, this much for letters. How can he eat when a horse cannot? How can he laugh when a horse is crying?

Our hero picks up his pen, wipes the tears from his eyes, and starts again. Quietly his words flow outward, etching refrains from others. Slowly, his passion ignites the hardened fabric of society's uncaring apathy. His heroism garners followers. Daniel daily enters the den of iniquity and grasps straws to weave a golden dream. That dream will shout to the heavens and shake the earth. Someday, horses will run free in the sun and wind. Beams from their glistening eyes and glorious peals of sound will carol off the clouds. Their very essence will create a freedom poem too beautiful to ignore, too profound to contain, and too complete to be other than sublime.

Sometime in the future, children will sit in rapt attention as the tales of heroes are told. One of those stories will be about a man named Daniel, who gave the horses back their poetry.

# Gabby (A Small Morality Play)

As my past becomes longer, drifting into the shadows of memory, I've come to the conclusion that true stupidity is an art form, which may take many years of concerted effort to refine into perfection. Consider the case of Gabby, a small palomino pony mare. Gabby was a schooling horse that delighted in teaching small children the art of walk/trot and, when they earned the privilege, some even cantered with wind-in-the-hair delight.

As we all must, Gabby increased in years and decreased in speed and agility. She belonged to a small 4-H club and was downgraded from being a "using" horse to a "used-up" horse. With limited stall space and no excess pasture, there was no room for her. Her owners decided to be kind, and, rather than offering her at auction, they placed a small ad in the local weekly free paper, something lighthearted about Gabby being "free to a good home." They pictured someone taking her for a companion animal or maybe a horse to do just a bit of light work with children. Into her life, however, came a hulking brute of a man, his bulk exceeding two hundred pounds, and the sight of his toes under his belly was a long-lost dream of his. He (let's call him Claude) promised to care for Gabby, agreed not to send her to the meat market, loaded her into a ramshackle trailer, and took her down the road. This should have ended the story other than a footnote about Gabby's sunset years of joy in Claude's barn and pastures. But Claude was a well-versed practitioner in the arts of stupidity, and there were to be no sunset years of joy for Gabby at his place.

Gabby is a very small horse, and even as a strong, sinewy three-year-old, a rider who weighed over two hundred pounds was over her weight limit. Most people (even the most un-horsey person around) would look and realize that a horse that small, that old, would not be able to carry a rotund adult male. But one of the facets of advanced stupidity is the inability to reason logically or even superficially. And as Claude had an advanced degree in stupidity (he should have worn one of those signs that Jeff Foxworthy suggests), the first thing he did when he got Gabby off the trailer was to throw an oversized western saddle on her back and climb on. She groaned, sagged, and then went down heavily. Claude hit the ground and rolled upright cussing, "I'll teach that no-count horse that she can't throw me and live." I will spare you the ensuing scene other than to remark that the sounds of pain filled the air so pervasively that no fewer than three of Claude's neighbors called the police on him.

When the police arrived, Gabby was sprawled in a heap across reddened ground, and Claude was sweating heavily from his exertions. Claude was well known to the local police as a wife beater, and they were not surprised his disdain of females had extended to this small mare. They coaxed her into a trailer and took her over to the local large animal impound. Claude also took a short trip over to the jail. The next day in court, Claude pleaded no contest to one count of animal cruelty (the joys of plea bargaining). Claude agreed to relinquish the horse, paid a two-hundred-dollar fine and was heard to mutter, "Don't need no no-count horse, no how," as the judge told him he would not be able to own another horse in this state for five years. Gabby ended up being trucked to The Last Refuge, as had so many other lost ones before her. She arrived here striped like a zebra (only her stripes were raw flesh) and in need of immediate surgery. The surgery was performed, the stripes healed, and Gabby was off to a new home with an adoring child to love and protect her from the stupidities of life. She resides there still and, although her fine hair is scarred, her heart beats as full of love as ever.

The moral of this telling might be expressed in the belief that true stupidity resides not just in the Claude's of this world but also in the people who placed Gabby into Claude's and his counterparts' eager hands.

# *The Many Shades of Gratitude*

Gratitude comes in many forms—some blatant enough as to be obvious to all but the sensory deprived, and others so tenuous as to leave the onlooker wondering. This is true not just with human interactions but with animals, as well. When is it gratitude and when is it just an extraneous response? Consider the following scenarios and answer for me, please, "Is it gratitude?"

Gabby, the horse in the previous episode, is a small palomino; she's just a hair above pony height. When she arrived at The Last Refuge, she had over one hundred sutures in her neck; her hips stretched skyward, and her ribs caved in enough to be in danger of touching in the middle. Her eyes were dull, and her coat was a conglomeration of crisscrossed whip marks and long-dead hair. Due to the nature of her neck injury, we were sure her lack of vocalization had a physical cause; we didn't worry that she was silent.

By the time she left here to go to her adoptive home, Gabby had gained weight, brightened up, and there was a small spring in her step. As she was loaded to go, she turned her mute gaze toward me and rubbed her head softly along my arm. I wiped away a tear and wished her well in her new home. A month later, when I went to visit, she came up to me and again rubbed along my arm as if she remembered me. I asked if she spoke at all and sadly heard the negative answer. We agreed, though, that her eyes showed happiness and that was enough. As I turned to leave, there was a soft, low sound behind me. From any other horse I would have considered it a whicker; from Gabby, however, it was a bellows. Startled, I turned to see her bow her head and softly say farewell again. She has not spoken since. Was that gratitude I heard? Or just a fluke?

Sling was a retired barrel racer, a huge, dark bay Morgan gelding. He was a "free to a good home" horse that came with the promise that he would not be shown again. He was extremely cold-backed and could drop to the ground if a cinch was tightened too suddenly. He also had no gait in between walk/jig and full-tilt running. His back sagged and his eyes drooped in conjunction with his lower lip. He looked and acted like a horse that had "been there, done that" and just wasn't going to do it anymore. The only thing that really motivated him was his love of carrots. After he had had an extended rest period on pasture, I attempted to see if he would enjoy doing a few quiet trail rides with his best friend along as a companion. Sling loved it; he was bright and alert, looking around and just plain having a grand time. I knew that trail rides were his forte when, after coming back, he took the offered carrot and, instead of eating it, he brought it to me and proudly dropped it into my hand. Was that gratitude? Or was he just not hungry?

At the last town fair, there was a section of the horse show events devoted to the beginning riders. I saw an Adult Beginner Class where an elderly horse was being shown in walk/trot with an obvious beginner, a grandmother type. The chestnut gelding had seen many miles and smelled of "overused schooling horse" in gait and manner. His rider was inexperienced, and it was obvious to all onlookers that the horse was obeying the judge's commands, and his passenger was just going along "for the ride." To no one's amazement, they didn't place and I halfway expected to see the usual disappointment after they left the show ring. To my happy surprise, the rider jumped down and proceeded to caress her horse with words and hands, declaring him to be the best out there, the finest mount in the world, and (punctuated with kisses and goodies) the winner of the show. The old, tired gelding arched his neck and softly blew pleasure back at her. The two together were the most content team I saw that day. They considered each other their true ribbon of award. I never found out the story behind them and was left wondering: Was that gratitude for their partnership? Or just a lack of competitiveness I saw?

Gratitude takes many forms, and some are so subtle as to leave only the finest texture of emotion to color the day. But then again, what is silk compared to wool and is either more a fabric than the other?

# *Humor*

Horses have an earthy sense of humor. Step in a bucket, and they'll chuckle at you. Fall down with it stuck on your foot, and they'll roar! Of course, if you hurt yourself, the humor is over, and they are immediately anxious, poking with their noses and nickering to make sure you're all right. Pratfalls are fine, but pain is another matter.

I was out in the barn tonight and bent over to fill the bathtub outside from the hose. The next thing I knew, Lady had lifted me carefully by the seat of my pants and deposited me into the tub. Wet and agitated, I looked up to see her grab the still-running hose and turn around, spraying the rest of the herd in the process. Now, that's what I call helping you to have fun.

Another favorite game is grabbing a towel in their teeth and chasing the rest of the herd across the field, waving it at them and attempting to slap their rumps with it. We call it flag faceball around here. When that pales, there's always tug of war with it, and when (not if) the towel rips, then it's twice the fun.

I have walked into the barn of a morning and seen all these heads turn toward me and a look that tells me they've plotted something: Don't turn my back on anyone…and, sure enough, someone "gets me" before the day is through. Some examples that flash through my mind and set me to chuckling are:

- Lady and Mike standing on either end of a drop-down bar that closes in the backyard entrance, looking at each other and somehow simultaneously lifting, then releasing the whole herd into the back yard and calling loudly to me to tell me about the "bad" horses!
- Patches slurping up water just before I go to clean his feet. The object of this game is to hold it in his mouth, then spit it down my back as I lift the first foot. This game produces the best results in the winter.
- A horse named Monkey could open any and all locks. He loved to let himself out at night and roam up and down the aisle teasing everyone else.

- Topaz would take a red cricket ball out into the field and stand around laughing as the others discovered the "apple" and tried to eat it. He still pulls this one on each new horse!

- The whole herd chases a little pony over the hill, screaming at him as he rolls under the fence and comes trotting up to the barn chuckling. (I never did find out what he pulled on them to make them so irate but he wasn't called the Tasmanian Devil for nothing.)

- Walking over the hills one day, I called for a horse that I was positive must be up a tree hiding, only to discover him quietly following me as I searched for him. He laughed, touched noses with me, flicked his tail, and ran off when I finally turned around to see him.

The most amazing thing about a horse's sense of humor is that he has one. All of the above horses came here out of "not great" lifestyles. Yet all have been able to reach within themselves and forgive, forget, and relearn joy, laughter, and hope. Maybe an earthy sense of humor is not such a bad thing to have.

# *Whoa*

Picture a horse sitting back on her heels and squatting with the effort to stop before she slides through a closed gate. On her back is an elderly man leaning back so far that his boots are tipped almost straight up in the stirrups. It is obvious from the glazed look in his eyes, he is convinced they are going through that gate and even his mustache is bunched up, trying to avoid the coming collision. As the inevitable approached, the mare sat the rest of the way down, and they teetered precariously together in front of the gate. The man sighed with relief; the mare turned and looked at him, then shook herself like a dog, stood up and waited for the gate to be opened, and eased on out afterward. This was not the winning barrel race of all time, but it was the last one that the cowboy tried to do using that mustang.

The barrel race was at a small 4-H club event, and we thought it was a good time to take the mare and let her be exposed to a crowd. She was convinced she did not want to go to the show. She was feeling extremely PMS (PO Mare Syndrome) that day, and it was all we could do to convince her she would enjoy herself. She stood and watched the other horse-and-rider teams race across the field, around the barrels and back, with a pronounced sneer on her face. It was touch and go whether she would go in when her turn was called, and frankly, to say she sauntered over to the barrels is to attribute more speed than was actually utilized. By the time she reached the first barrel, it was obvious that an amble was as much enthusiastic momentum as she was willing to expend. The man leaned back, allowed her to stroll on out and was prepared for just as leisurely a return to the gate. This is where the grand-slam slide home described in the first paragraph occurred. The mustang had figured out that where she went in, she could also exit, and she was a lot more interested in a quick finale than anyone, including her rider, was prepared for.

So many of us are guilty of the same thing—rushing out the in-door in our haste to get things over with and done. The modern, prepackaged world has taught us to expect immediate results, and if they're not forthcoming, we tend to throw up our hands and leave by the same way we came in. We've forgotten that the beauty lies within the journey itself and an ending is just that.

This particular barn chat will therefore have no ending, just a request that as you journey through my barn, and on into the rest of your life, you carry some of the beauty that is inherent in my "babies" with you to savor and smile over now and then. And if you choose to go out the in-door, please wait long enough for someone to open it for you.

# *All Horses Are Brown, Aren't They?*

The English language is an amazing creation. We have everyday terms that are taken for granted which, when you stop and think, have underlying shades of meaning. For example, we talk about people as being sports mad, bitten by the reading bug, crazy about horses, and so forth. Depending on the speaker, those expressions take on whole new concepts and mental pictures. Well, just look at what can be meant by "crazy about horses." I've been called that, and you can be sure that it wasn't always meant as a compliment.

We just love to categorize each other, so there are "horse" people and "non-horse" people out there, and being in one or the other category is not predicated by whether or not one owns a horse or not.

I would never presume to classify someone as being a "horsey" or "non-horsey" person, but I can certainly provide examples of things that have been said to me and define what category the words belong in. Running an animal rescue facility, which allows some limited public visitation, has certainly exposed me to both. And will you be surprised if I tell you some of the worst offenders—from a horse's standpoint—are owners of them?

"Well, they're not *real* horses. They're so small and ugly—no wonder they got dumped. Who would want them?" These were some of the comments made by a group of young girls from an upscale Equine Training Barn (English Hunter-Jumper set) upon viewing my latest collection of rag-tag tattered discards. Definitely non-horsey comments.

"I thought all horses were brown" came from a small child staring with wide-eyed wonder at a herd of multi-colored horses (my paint brigade). This comment could go either way—but oh, the look. That child was horsey, to be sure.

Okay now, I'll recite the quote and you decide the category. Ready?

"What kind of warranty do they come with? You don't expect me to adopt a less than perfect one, do you? I couldn't be bothered with a (choose one) _____ (lame, ugly, old, sway-backed, and so forth) one." I heard this one many times from people calling to inquire about adoption possibilities.

"Well, what *good* are they to you? How come you keep the ones no one else wants? Don't they just take up valuable space?" Same reference as above.

"Please take my horse. I'm dying of cancer, and none of my kids want him. I know my son will sell him at auction as soon as I'm dead. He's told me so." This came from an elderly man as he cried and unloaded his old horse into my barn.

"You better have a bill of sale for that horse or be willing to cough up some bucks. He's worth money to me." This comment came over the phone from his son the next day. (I ended up paying him $200, meat price, to go away and leave the horse with me.)

"Isn't he the most beautiful horse in the world!" This one came from a nine-year-old whose parents had just given her an adopted chestnut-colored gelding with bad legs and a scar down his nose.

"My Chester may not be the most beautiful horse in the world, but no one will ever love a horse as much as I love him. Or be loved as much as he loves me." This one came from same girl at eleven.

"She's had both her flexor tendons severed; she'll never be rideable. She has no papers, and her personality is not the world's best. Okay, Carol, don't look at me that way. I'll do the surgery and cast the leg. Pay me what you can." This came from my vet upon being presented with a quarter horse/Arab mare that someone had tried to hamstring.

"Well, would you look at her float across the field! She moves like a dream, doesn't she? Never believe what she'd been through. Of course, she still doesn't have the best personality, heheheh." My vet said this about the same horse six months later, the same one that he's never "gotten around" to writing a bill for.

"Doesn't it just smell like heaven in here?" This was happily chirped by a twenty-year-old Down's syndrome friend as he cleaned out a stall.

"What I like best about horses is they like me; no one else does." This was whispered to an elderly horse by a fourteen-year-old "terror" who had been remanded to work off community service in my barn.

"Don't flinch. No one is ever going to hurt you anymore. Calm, quiet—that's the key. Easy, easy, boy. You're safe here. Well, aren't you just the most beautiful horse in the world? Here's a hug for you." The same "terror" said this while working with an extremely abused horse that would shake and fall down screaming if you went in the stall with him.

"I passed all my classes! Now keep your promise! Comet is mine!" I heard this from the same child about the same horse one year later.

"Listen to him call to me! Better get busy and do my chores. Comet wants me to groom him afterward." Now seventeen, this "terror" is still in school and works here to cover Comet's needs. The two of them are going to be just fine together, I can tell.

Done categorizing? For me, a "horsey" person is one with compassion, an open-eyed wonder at the joys of life, and an ability to reach outside of themselves to share with another being. I don't care whether that being has two legs, four legs, none, or more (well, some of those more can be pretty "yucky"). The ability to reach out and offer comfort defines a "horsy" person to me. What do you think?

# *Sanctuary*

Earlier today, I was talking with Jerry, the director of Habitat for Horses, and we were discussing the different paths we both follow. His mission has broadened to include working closely with the police and judicial departments of Galveston County, and his volunteers are all dedicated to rescuing and rehabilitating immediate-needs cases, rather than the long-term ones. Although I volunteer at Habitat and assist with rescues, I'm not an official rescue person. Instead, I offer sanctuary to special-needs animals, those that have no other place to go. Jerry and I have accepted the fact that our surrounding counties will always need active rescue workers, as well as sanctuary workers, as options for horses, donkeys, and mules.

Jerry and I are often asked about the differences between rescue work and sanctuary duties. For starters, my place, The Last Refuge, is a sanctuary, a nebulous term that can leave some people confused. I can't speak for all sanctuaries, but I can explain what mine is like. Again, I'm not a "rescue"; I don't wear the badge, and I'm not called in when horses are found neglected and abused, but I am fortunate enough to be in the same town as Jerry's Habitat for Horses, a model for all that a rescue should be.

Rescue deals with immediate crises—the face-to-face confrontations with callous, belligerent owners, the loading of mistreated horses, and taking them to safety. Rescue personnel deal with these situations daily. It is stressful, tense labor that is poorly understood and rarely appreciated by people outside the immediate rescue circle. Many of the rewards that the rest of us take for granted, as part of our work, are not given to rescue workers. The major, headline-making cases fade from people's memories often before the paper they are printed on can be recycled, while rescue workers are continuing to clean up, patch, repair, and go on to the next rescue effort. Rescues exist to rescue, and I bow my head in humble gratitude for their presence.

After endangered equines are transferred to safety, the rescue team is faced with a triage of problems. Each horse must be evaluated, and choices must be made. This one will be rehabilitated and will end up sound; that one is perfect for light riding; and these can be earmarked for a therapy program. Basically, the list settles down into choices.

Like small children picking sides for a game, the pool of horses is divided, and it dwindles as the selection continues. However, there is at least one, and sometimes more than one, that isn't picked. Perhaps the animal is too small, too blind, too slow, too lame, or too ugly; the reasons are as numerous as they can be vague. In the end, both the children choosing team players and the horse selectors are left with some that just don't fall into any category. Cast off and ignored, they stand, watching the others play and wondering what part of them was too wrong to be picked. "Sanctuary," they cry, "we need a place of refuge and protection. Safety is needed by the last as well as by the first." Those are the ones I want. My sanctuary's name, The Last Refuge, is an expression of that belief; it is a secure place of safety, a place for the last ones.

What is a sanctuary? The Last Refuge is a forever home for the ones not picked, for that last horse who is waiting—the lame, the old, the needy, and yes, even the cranky. It doesn't matter to me if they're sway-backed, lame, or toothless. My sanctuary is here for them as a source of help, relief, and comfort, a place of refuge and protection.

# *On the Porch*

Chipper, Bailer, and I have just come in from the porch, where Duke, my porch ornament donkey, is happily ensconced, munching on hay. He came up to share the moment, and he lingered to enjoy the pleasure of having a freshly dog-washed face. Together, the four of us watched the sunset, sharing in the silent harmony of a day almost done. The week has faded into a small montage of images that poke incessantly at me, as Chip often does, to tell their stories.

- **Gracie and Chase**: two bonded siblings, two chocolate-sweetness Labs, who have gone to a loving home after being unceremoniously discarded like last year's fashion error.
- **Snowbell**: an elderly horse, finally able to chew after a long-overdue dental procedure, is rediscovering the joys of un-chopped hay—and my food processor is also enjoying the respite.
- **Darby**: a horse who came here with a broken vertebrae still amazes me, as I look out the window and see a horse walking without stumbling for the first time in months.

On my way home, I stopped by Habitat for Horses, to take a look at yet another of Jerry's "Stop by, Carol, I have something for you to see" horses. This one will be a difficult case. Tears on both our parts punctuated Jerry's low, whispered discussion, but the hook was firmly set. Now, through the haze of setting dusk, I see a new silken thread, drawing me toward a new baby that will come here tomorrow, come home tomorrow to The Last Refuge.

# *Glossary*

**Backyard horse**   A horse that lives with its owner. Some people consider that the ideal existence; for others, however, they look down it, criticizing the owner for not providing a "proper barn or stable" for the horse.

**Bale**   A measurement of hay, equal to 10 "flakes" of about 5–7 pounds each. Depending on the weather, a horse can consume a third of a bale or more each day.

**Barn sour**   A horse that doesn't like to leave the barn or stable.

**Bombproof**   A horse that doesn't spook easily. A priceless horse for beginners and small children, they are often overlooked for flashy, hot-blooded alternatives.

**Cannon bone**   A bone in a horse that extends from the knee (or hock) to the fetlock.

**Chestnut**   A brownish-yellow coat color. A chestnut horse's mane and tail are usually the same color as the coat. An alternative definition of **chestnut** refers to the little oval of hard, rough skin found mid-way up the inside of all four legs. In Western riding, a chestnut is often called a sorrel.

**Cold bloods**   A designation for any horse or breed of horse without Arabian or Eastern blood in its breeding. In practice, since many so-called cold-blooded breeds have been improved by the use of Arab blood, the distinction is based mainly on physical type; broadly speaking, all heavy draft horses and most European native ponies are classed as cold bloods.

**Colt**   An ungelded male horse up to four years old.

**Conformation**   The structure and general make-up of a horse.

**Coronet**   The small area that attaches the hoof to the rest of the leg.

**Crest**   The area between the poll and the withers.

**Dorsal stripe**  A colored stripe, usually black or brown, running down the back of the horse, from the mane and continuing into the tail.

**Dished**  A term referring to the concave profile of a horse's head, such as that of an Arabian horse.

**Dun**  A yellow coat with black mane, tail, legs, and a dorsal stripe.

**Farrier**  A person trained professionally to tend to horses' hooves.

**Feather**  The hair on the back of cannon bones and around a horse's fetlocks.

**Fetlock**  The lowest joint in a horse's leg.

**Filly**  A female horse up to four years of age.

**Floating teeth**  A horse dentist "floats teeth" (rasps them), filing off the sharp points and keeping the chewing surfaces in proper contact with each other.

**Foal**  A horse of any gender, up to one year old.

**Forehand/Forequarters**  Collectively, the head, neck, shoulders, withers, and forelegs of a horse.

**Frog**  The V-shaped area found on the bottom of horses' hooves.

**Gait**  A reference to the paces at which a horse moves. Common gaits are walking, trotting, cantering and galloping, although there are more in different breeds.

**Galls**  Sores caused by poorly fitting tack; also called saddle sores.

**Gelding**  A castrated male horse.

**Gray**  Any color from pure white to dark gray.

**Groom**  A person who looks after a horse; also called a stable hand. **Groom** can also be a verb, referring to the act of brushing and cleaning a horse.

**Hand**  A unit of measurement to determine the height of a horse. 1 hand = 4 inches.

**Hard keeper**   A horse whose weight is hard to maintain.

**Hinny**   The sterile offspring of a male horse (a stallion) and a female donkey (a jennet).

**Hock**   The joint in the center part of a horse's hind legs.

**Hooves**   Horses' "feet."

**Horn**   The hard, insensitive outer part of a hoof.

**Hot bloods**   Horses of Arab or other Eastern descent.

**Irons**   An English riding term referring to metal items that are attached to a saddle by pieces of leather used to hold riders' feet.

**Jack donkey**   Used interchangeably with **donkey jack**, the term refers to a male donkey.

**Jennet**   A female donkey.

**John mule**   A male mule.

**Knee-Up/Leg Up**   A way of mounting a horse that requires two people; one person helps the other onto the horse by taking their knee in the palm of the helper's hands and lifting them off the ground.

**Leathers**   Another English riding term, this one refers to the straps that hold the irons onto the saddle. A rider adjusts these so they are the proper length for their legs.

**Mammoth draft mule**   A mule that has a draft mare (Belgium or Percheron, for example) for a mother and a mammoth jack donkey for a father.

**Mammoth jack**   A giant breed of donkeys started in North America by George Washington, who used a breeding pair given to him by the King of Spain.

**Mare**   A female horse over four years of age.

**Molly mule**   A female mule.

**Mount**  Getting up onto the horse. You can mount from the ground, a mounting block, or by getting a knee-up.

**Mucking out**  Removing dirty bedding and replacing it with clean bedding.

**Mule**  The offspring of a mare and a jack donkey.

**Near side**  The left side of a horse; also the side you mount from.

**Palomino**  Various shades of gold. A palomino horse has a white mane and tail.

**Poll**  The area between a horse's ears.

**Pommel**  The extreme front of a saddle.

**Pony**  A small horse measuring 14.2 hands high or less.

**Shy**  A term used to refer to a horse that jumps to the side when it's scared by something real or imaginary.

**Tack**  A term for all saddlery—that is, the saddle, the reins, the bit, and so forth.

**Throatlatch**  The underside of a horse's jaw, where it meets the neck.

**Ungelded**  An uncastrated horse; a stallion.

**Vice**  Any bad habit learned by a horse—for example, head tossing and rearing.

**Walleye**  An eye in which the iris, usually a pale translucent blue due to lack of pigment, is ringed with white.

**Warm bloods**  A designation for any horse or breed of horse with Arabian or Eastern blood in its breeding. In practice, the distinction is based mainly on physical type. Broadly speaking, all light saddle horses and harness horses are classed as warm bloods.

**Weanling**  A horse under one year old that has been weaned from his mother.

**Withers**  A point at the bottom of the neck, usually characterized by a slightly raised area, just above the shoulders. The saddle lays just behind this. A horse's height is measured from the ground to the withers.

# Afterword:
# Ending a National Disgrace

✦

## Legislative Efforts to End the Slaughter of American Horses

*By Christopher J. Heyde, Society for Animal Protective Legislation*

Unbeknownst to most Americans, tens of thousands of horses are annually hauled from all over the country to Texas and one of the two remaining U.S. based foreign-owned slaughter facilities. There, they are turned into meat and then sold as a delicacy in France, Italy, and Japan. Another estimated 30,000 are trucked to Canada and Mexico or flown to Japan for slaughter to meet the same fate.

Until recently the horse slaughter industry operated in virtual anonymity and they enjoyed this unknown status. Antiquated phrases such as "taking a trip to the glue factory" or "turned into dog food" were all that most thought remained of an outdated practice, but few people in America knew horses were continuing to be slaughtered for human consumption. This allowed the industry middlemen, known as "killer-buyers," to travel from auction to auction purchasing any horse they could, including thoroughbreds, workhorses, miniatures, and ponies, Premarin foals born as a "by-product" of the Premarin industry, federally protected wild horses, and companion animals.

Once in the hands of the killer-buyers, horses are subjected to unimaginable cruelty. Every step facing the unfortunate horses purchased by the industry consists of unimaginable suffering for the horses. A Pennsylvania Police Equine Investigator from the New Holland Livestock Auction stated in *The Horse* magazine that, "...horses were deprived of food and water because they were going to slaughter anyway. My conclusion is that the slaughter option encourages neglect.... Money is the only objective of selling horses to slaughter." In the slaughterhouse, the suffering continues. Poorly trained and callous workers have been seen beating horses indiscriminately with thick fiberglass rods. Finally, often because of improper and inadequate efforts to render them insensitive to pain prior to slaughter, horses may be dismembered while still conscious.

While a few horse "industry" organizations remain opposed to the humane treatment of horses, they are in the minority, most likely ignoring their membership, and do so for economic interests. Their claims, that slaughter is a humane ending for suffering horses, does not sit well with the overwhelming majority of the American public. A survey conducted in Texas in May 2003 found that 89 percent of Texans had no idea horses were slaughtered for human consumption. It went on to report that 72 percent supported a ban on horse slaughter. If is fair to say that this survey, coming from the state with the largest horse population, is reflective of opinion throughout the U.S.

As public awareness has increased, horse slaughter has steadily declined from well over 300,000 horses in the early 1990s to just over 40,000 in 2002. While horses enjoy a unique place in American culture, little has been done to protect them from the deceitful practices used by the horse slaughter industry.

Outside of a hodgepodge of state laws such as a 1949 Texas state law prohibiting the sale, possession, and transport of horsemeat for human consumption, horse slaughter itself went unchecked until the 1970s. It wasn't until 1971, when the federal government responding to the public's outcry over the barbaric treatment and systematic eradication of America's wild horses, passed the Wild Free-Roaming Horses and Burros Act, which states "It is the policy of Congress that wild free-roaming horses and burros shall be protected from capture, branding, harassment, or death." Despite congressional intent, recent findings uncovered in an ongoing lawsuit to protect them, revealed that hundreds of wild horses are being sent to slaughter each year.

Then in 1985 an amendment was passed by the U.S. Congress outlawing the transport of horses by boat. Similar to what occurred with the Wild Horse Act, this law was also found to have been violated by a Washington State transport company in 2001. Although the Department of Commerce initiated their first investigation into this abuse at that time, it was readily evident the practice was of a longstanding nature.

The first specific effort to protect all equine from slaughter was a successful 1998 California ballot initiative banning the slaughter and transport of horses for slaughter in the state. While horse slaughter in California was not a thriving industry, the vote sent a powerful message about the cruel fate suffered by countless horses. In 2002, a similar initiative was attempted in Massachusetts, but because of signature gathering fraud perpetrated against the organizers, it was not included on the ballot.

In order to effectively address the slaughter problem, a federal law is necessary. In February 2003, Congressman John Sweeney (R-NY) and Congressman John Spratt (D-SC) introduced the American Horse Slaughter Prevention Act. This legislation, when enacted, will prevent the slaughter of horses within the U.S. and prohibit the export of live horses intended for slaughter. The bill enjoys broad support from horse rescue groups and national and local animal protection organizations as well as national and state horse industry groups such as The Breeders' Cup Ltd., NY Racing Association and Fasig-Tipton, Inc.—America's oldest thoroughbred auction house. The National Thoroughbred Racing Association has issued a statement supporting a ban, as have other leaders in the horse industry.

As the American Horse Slaughter Prevention Act gained momentum nationally, two efforts to defend the industry began in Texas. In 2002, the Texas Attorney General issued an opinion reaffirming the 1949 state law banning the sale and possession of horsemeat for human consumption, effectively rendering the industry illegal. As a result, local prosecutors initiated investigations into the operations of the Texas slaughter facilities. Almost immediately the slaughterhouses joined forces with another company in Mexico to file a lawsuit in federal court attempting to stop the state's enforcement efforts. At the same time, legislation was introduced in the Texas House of Representatives to overturn the 1949 law. However, the bill met with overwhelming opposition from Texans and was soundly rejected by the Senate—twice. In the meantime, the slaughterhouses are still operating pending a ruling on their request for a permanent injunction from the federal judge.

There is no defense for this industry. Horse slaughter is simply another form of animal cruelty that can be halted with the passage of the American Horse Slaughter Prevention Act. Once achieved, those concerned with the humane treatment of horses can refocus their attention to reducing the neglect and other forms of abuse that horses continue to face every day.

0-595-74923-2

Printed in the United States
94001LV00004B/27/A

**Dorsal stripe**   A colored stripe, usually black or brown, running down the back of the horse, from the mane and continuing into the tail.

**Dished**   A term referring to the concave profile of a horse's head, such as that of an Arabian horse.

**Dun**   A yellow coat with black mane, tail, legs, and a dorsal stripe.

**Farrier**   A person trained professionally to tend to horses' hooves.

**Feather**   The hair on the back of cannon bones and around a horse's fetlocks.

**Fetlock**   The lowest joint in a horse's leg.

**Filly**   A female horse up to four years of age.

**Floating teeth**   A horse dentist "floats teeth" (rasps them), filing off the sharp points and keeping the chewing surfaces in proper contact with each other.

**Foal**   A horse of any gender, up to one year old.

**Forehand/Forequarters**   Collectively, the head, neck, shoulders, withers, and forelegs of a horse.

**Frog**   The V-shaped area found on the bottom of horses' hooves.

**Gait**   A reference to the paces at which a horse moves. Common gaits are walking, trotting, cantering and galloping, although there are more in different breeds.

**Galls**   Sores caused by poorly fitting tack; also called saddle sores.

**Gelding**   A castrated male horse.

**Gray**   Any color from pure white to dark gray.

**Groom**   A person who looks after a horse; also called a stable hand. **Groom** can also be a verb, referring to the act of brushing and cleaning a horse.

**Hand**   A unit of measurement to determine the height of a horse. 1 hand = 4 inches.

# *Glossary*

**Backyard horse**   A horse that lives with its owner. Some people consider that the ideal existence; for others, however, they look down it, criticizing the owner for not providing a "proper barn or stable" for the horse.

**Bale**   A measurement of hay, equal to 10 "flakes" of about 5–7 pounds each. Depending on the weather, a horse can consume a third of a bale or more each day.

**Barn sour**   A horse that doesn't like to leave the barn or stable.

**Bombproof**   A horse that doesn't spook easily. A priceless horse for beginners and small children, they are often overlooked for flashy, hot-blooded alternatives.

**Cannon bone**   A bone in a horse that extends from the knee (or hock) to the fetlock.

**Chestnut**   A brownish-yellow coat color. A chestnut horse's mane and tail are usually the same color as the coat. An alternative definition of **chestnut** refers to the little oval of hard, rough skin found mid-way up the inside of all four legs. In Western riding, a chestnut is often called a sorrel.

**Cold bloods**   A designation for any horse or breed of horse without Arabian or Eastern blood in its breeding. In practice, since many so-called cold-blooded breeds have been improved by the use of Arab blood, the distinction is based mainly on physical type; broadly speaking, all heavy draft horses and most European native ponies are classed as cold bloods.

**Colt**   An ungelded male horse up to four years old.

**Conformation**   The structure and general make-up of a horse.

**Coronet**   The small area that attaches the hoof to the rest of the leg.

**Crest**   The area between the poll and the withers.